Thank you for your purchase!!

Flowers A to Z is an adult coloring book series designed to bring a little nature into your life. Created to help provide relaxation and stress relief, this book delivers hours of satisfying, entertaining fun while allowing you to express your innermost creative self. The drawings offer a nice range in detail and complexity allowing hours of enjoyment for everyone from beginners to experts.

The beautiful designs are all printed single sided to help prevent any color bleeding from one picture to another. However, if you are using markers, we do suggest that you place a single sheet of blank paper behind the page you are coloring.

If you enjoy your coloring experience please show your appreciation by leaving us a review. We would also love to see a picture of how your art has turned out!!

Flowers from A to Z

Volume 1

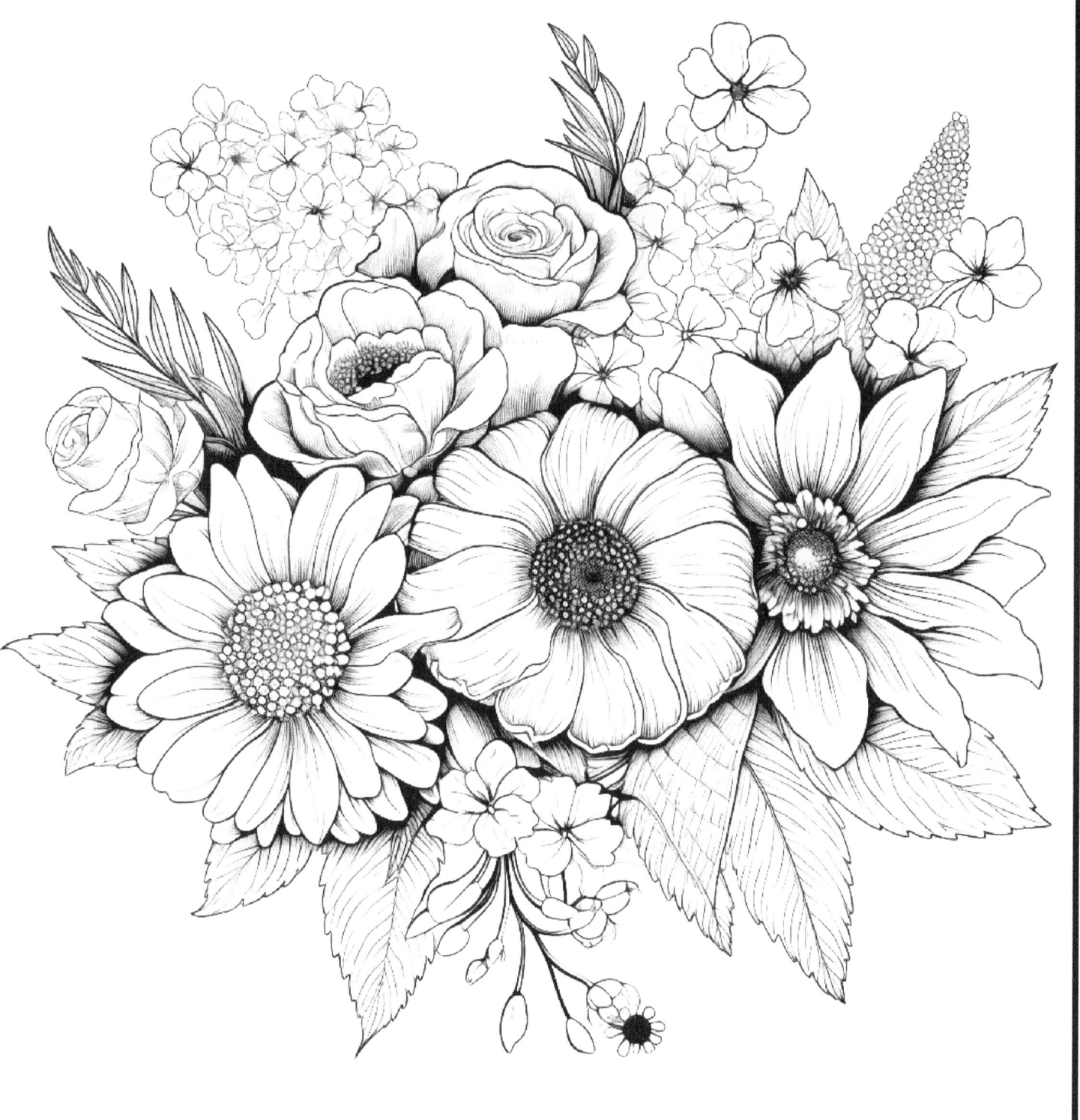

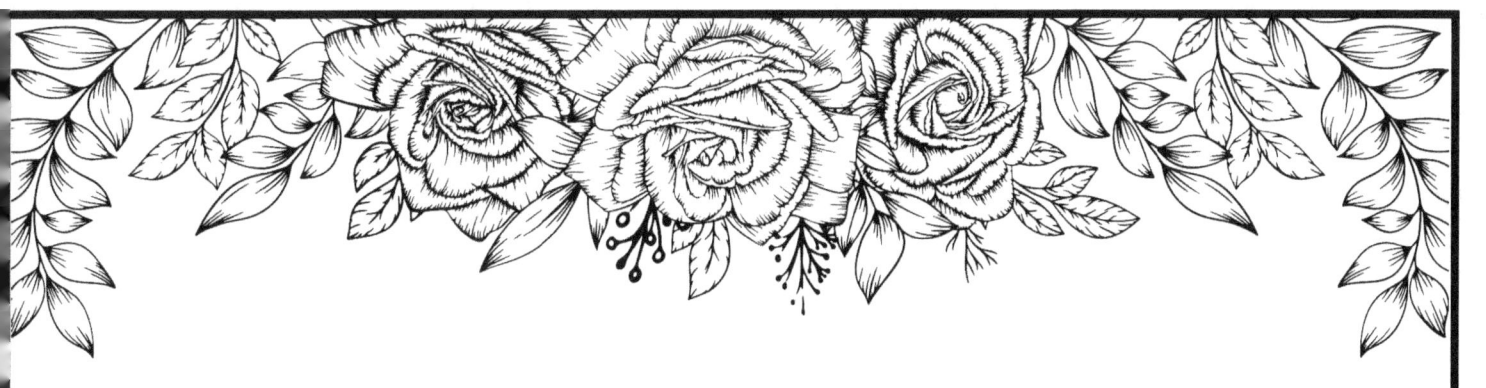

This book belongs to:

_____

_____

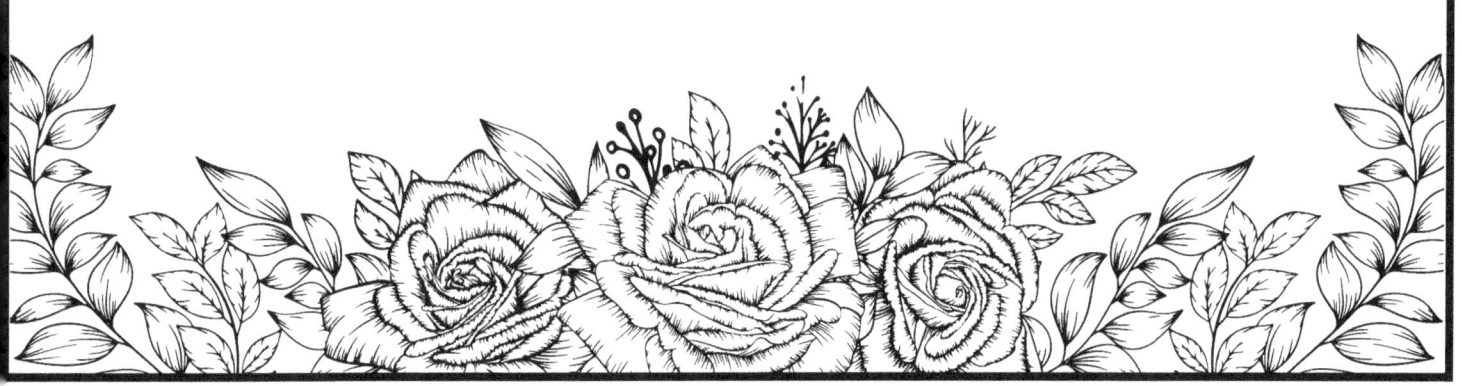

Color Testing

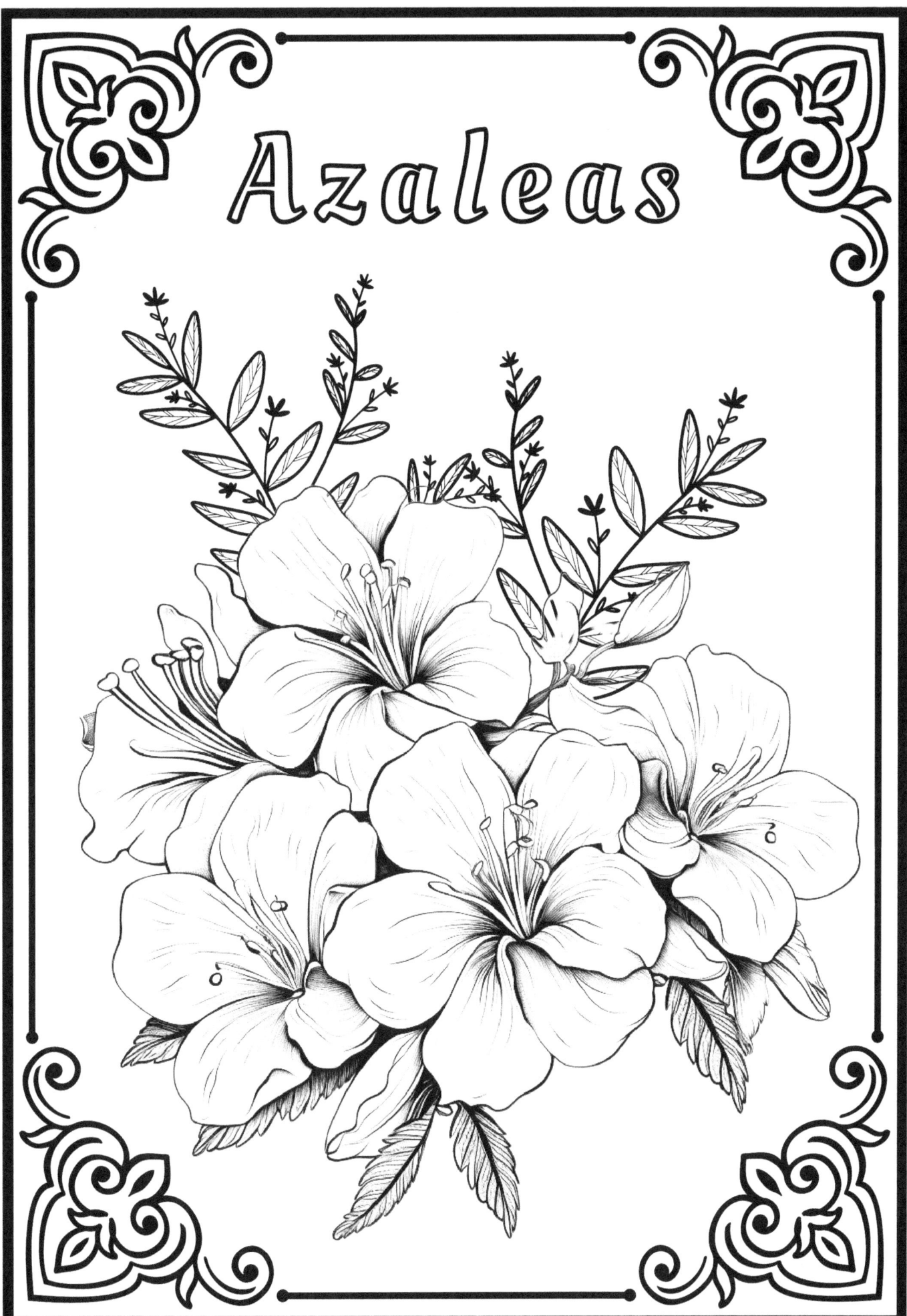

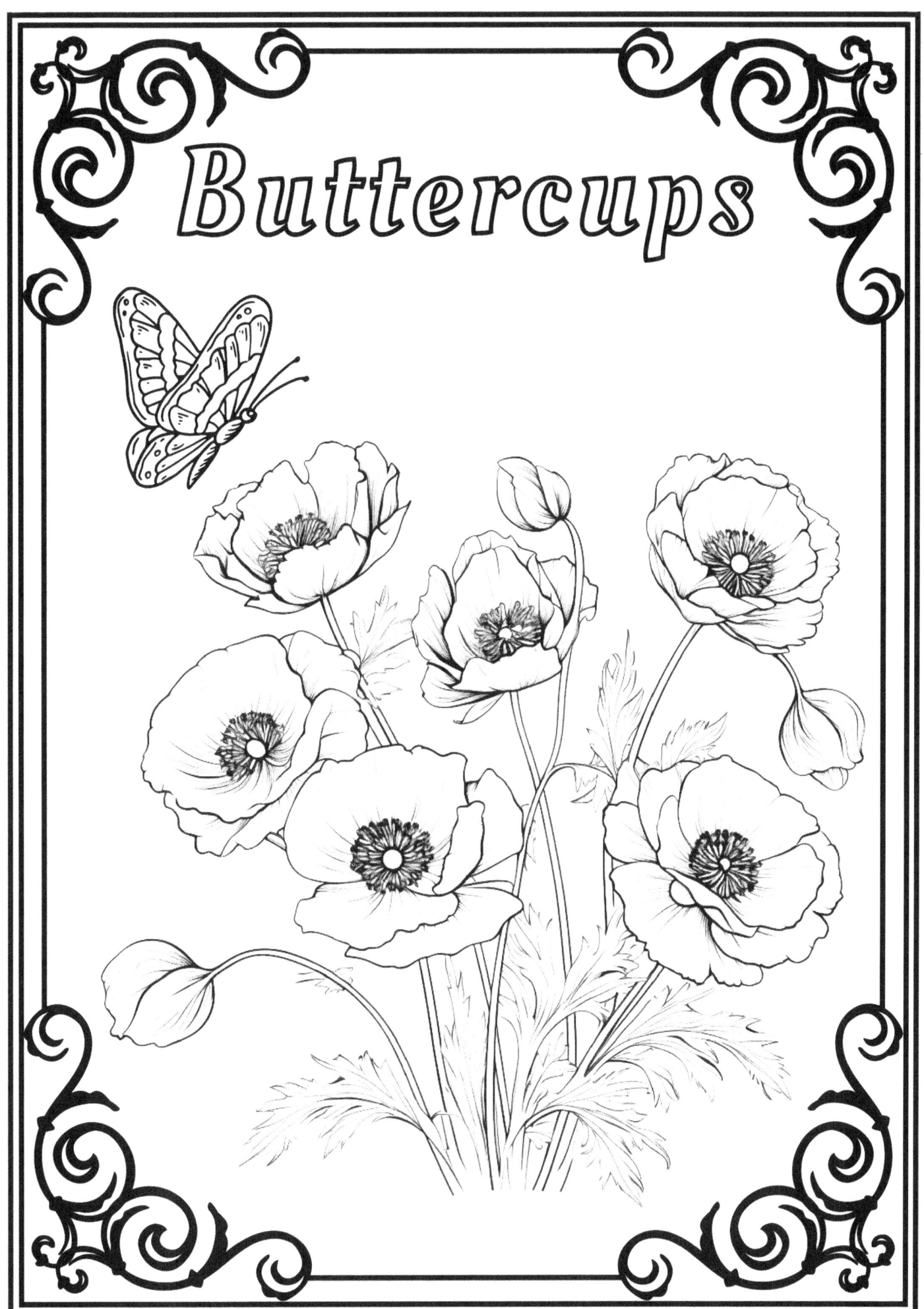

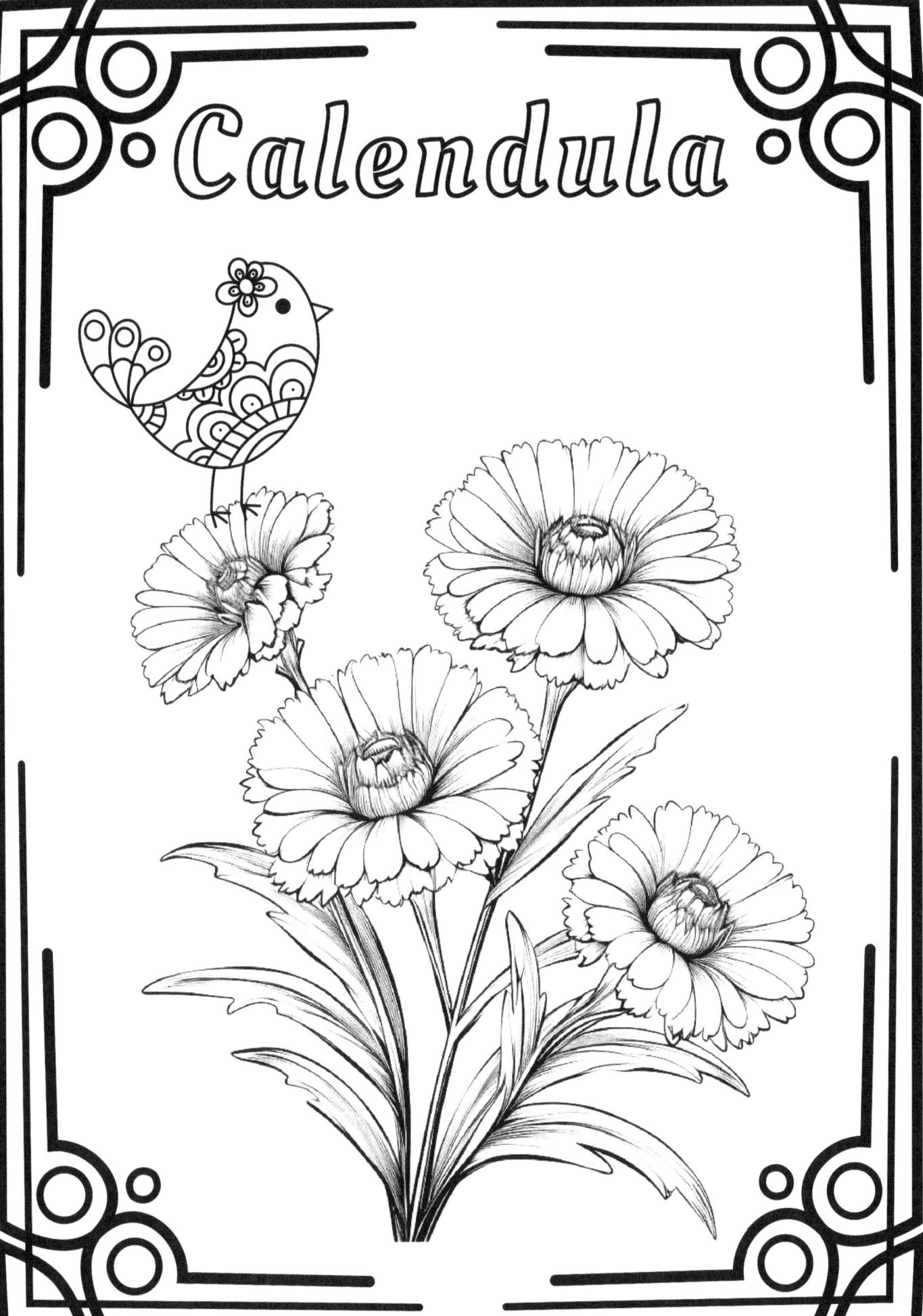

Calendula

Daisies

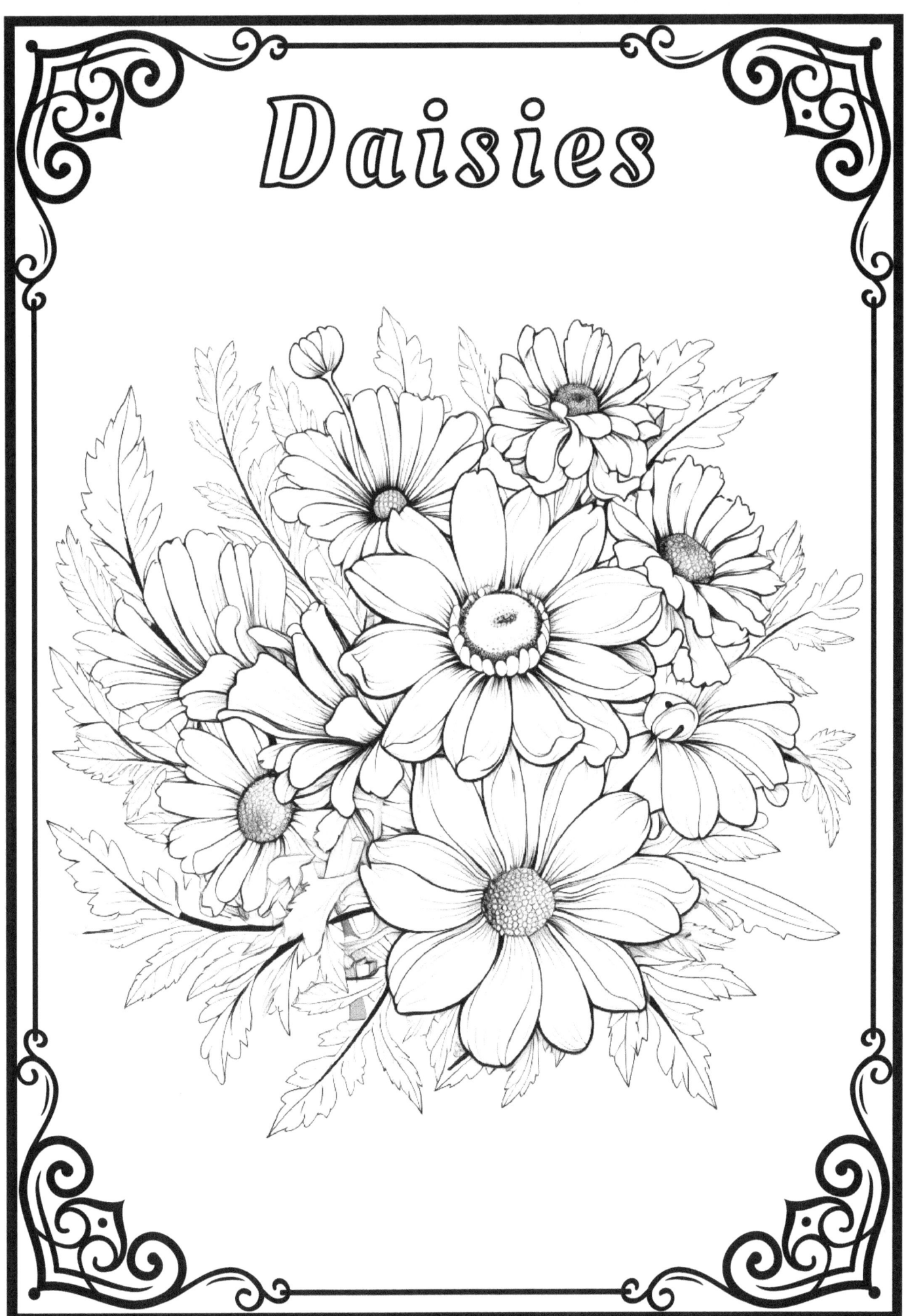

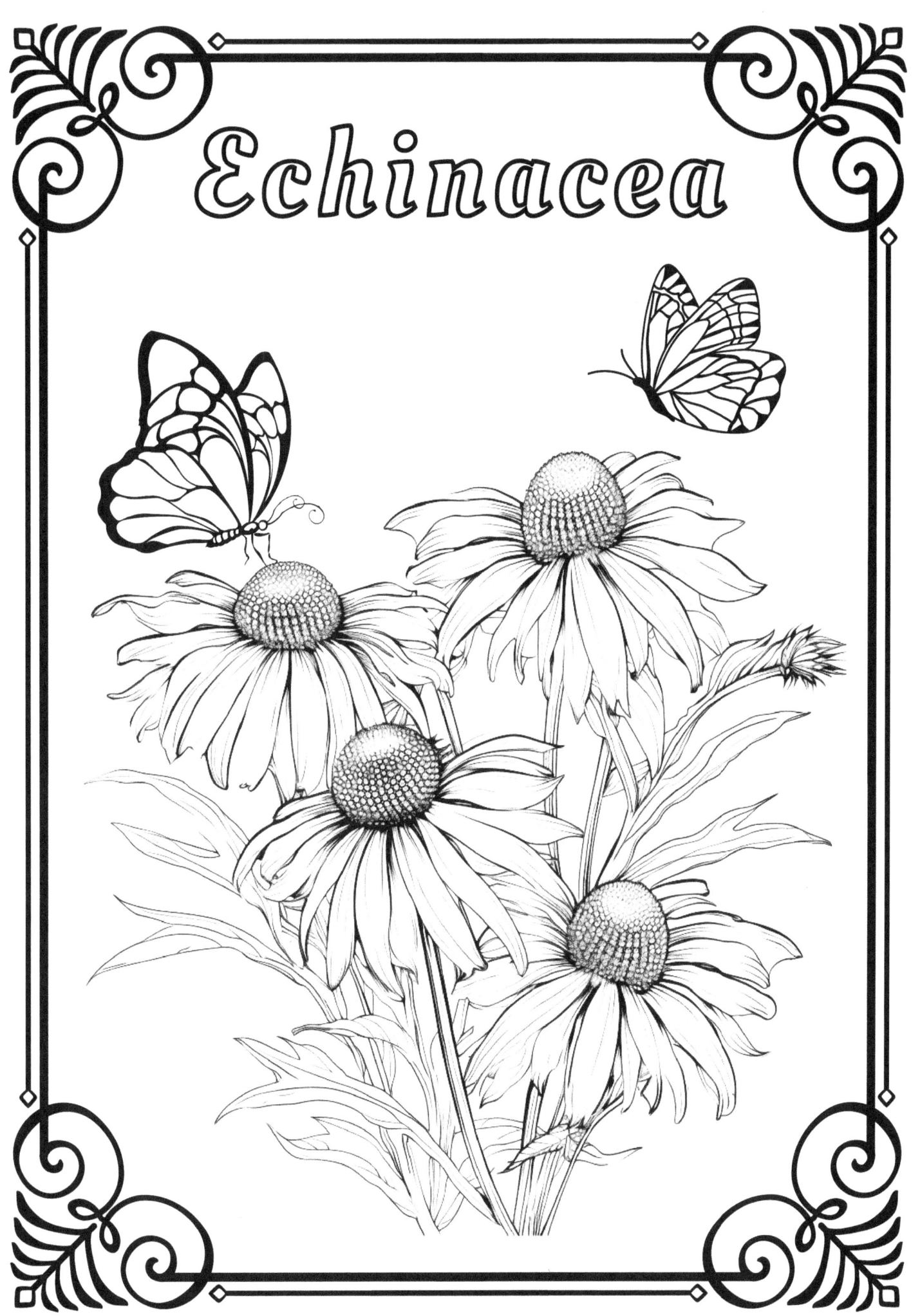

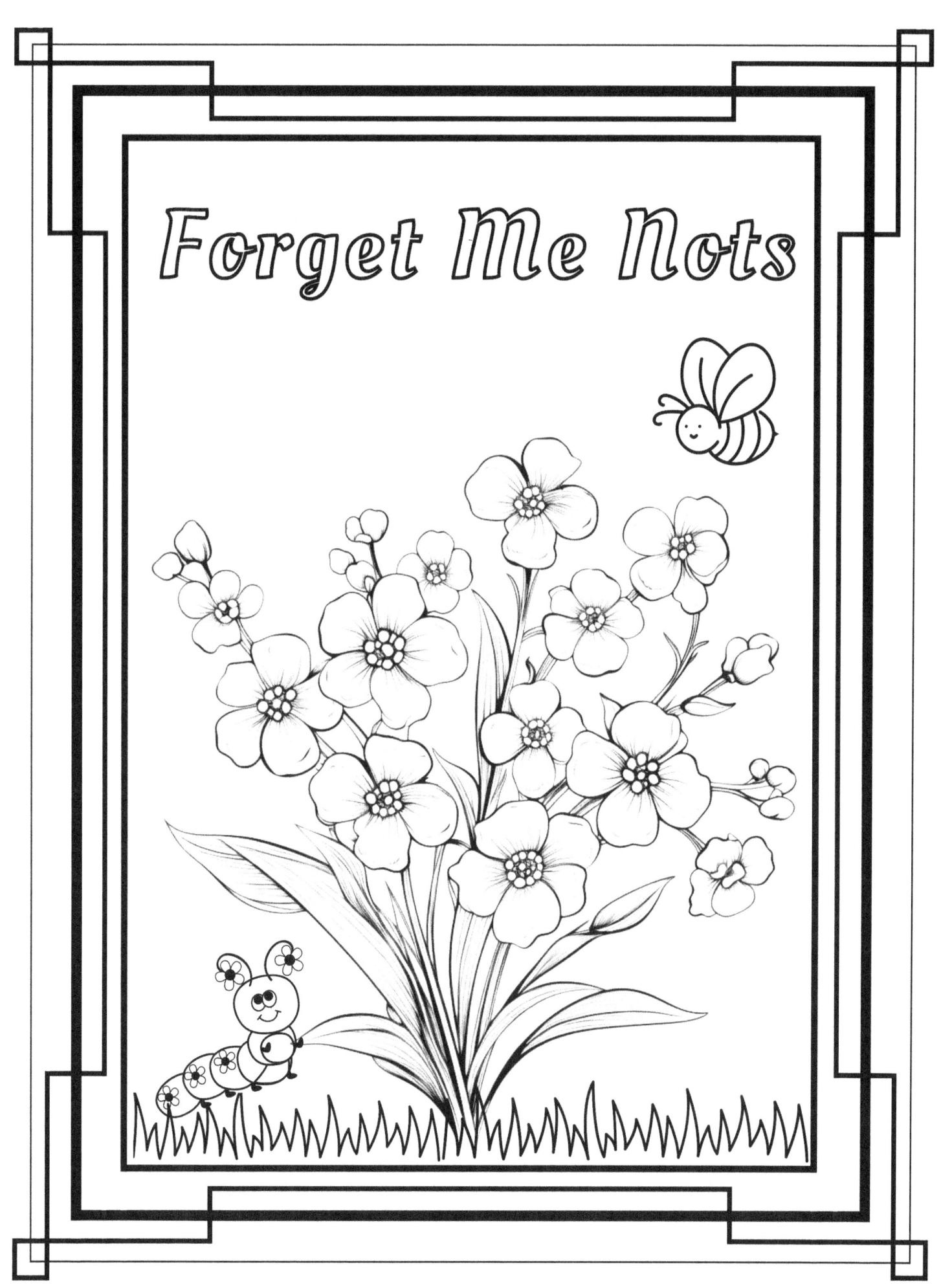

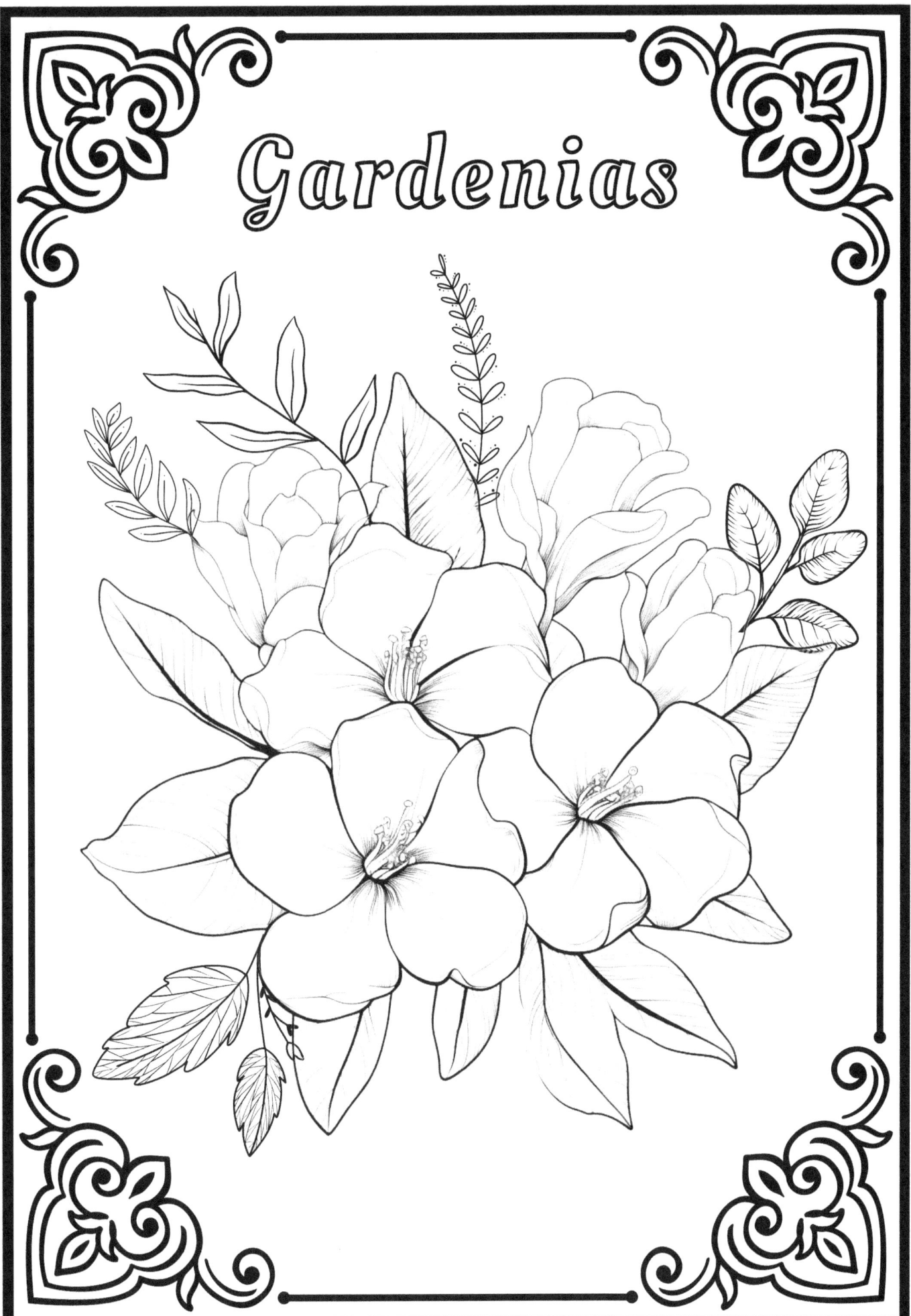

Gardenias

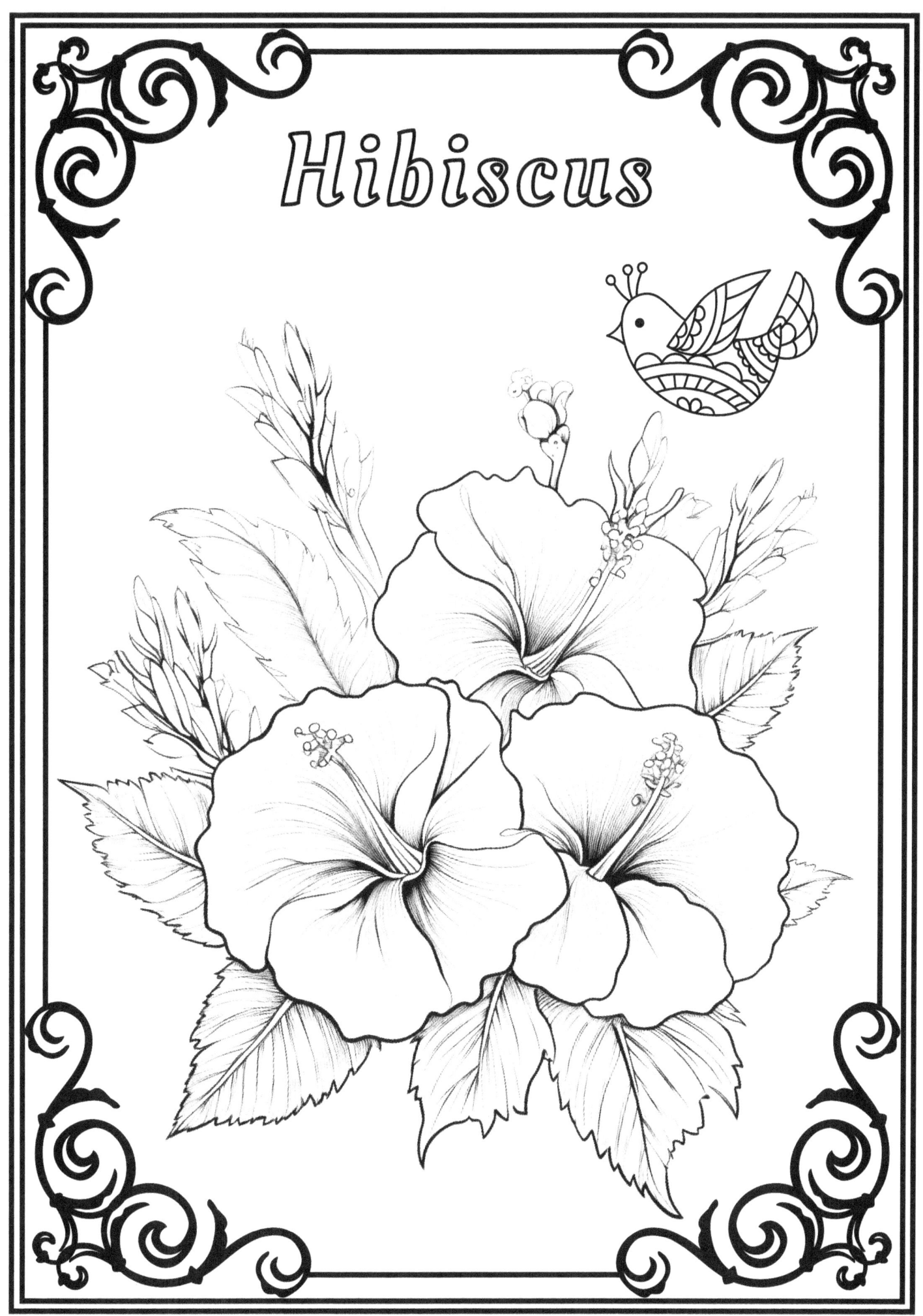

Hibiscus

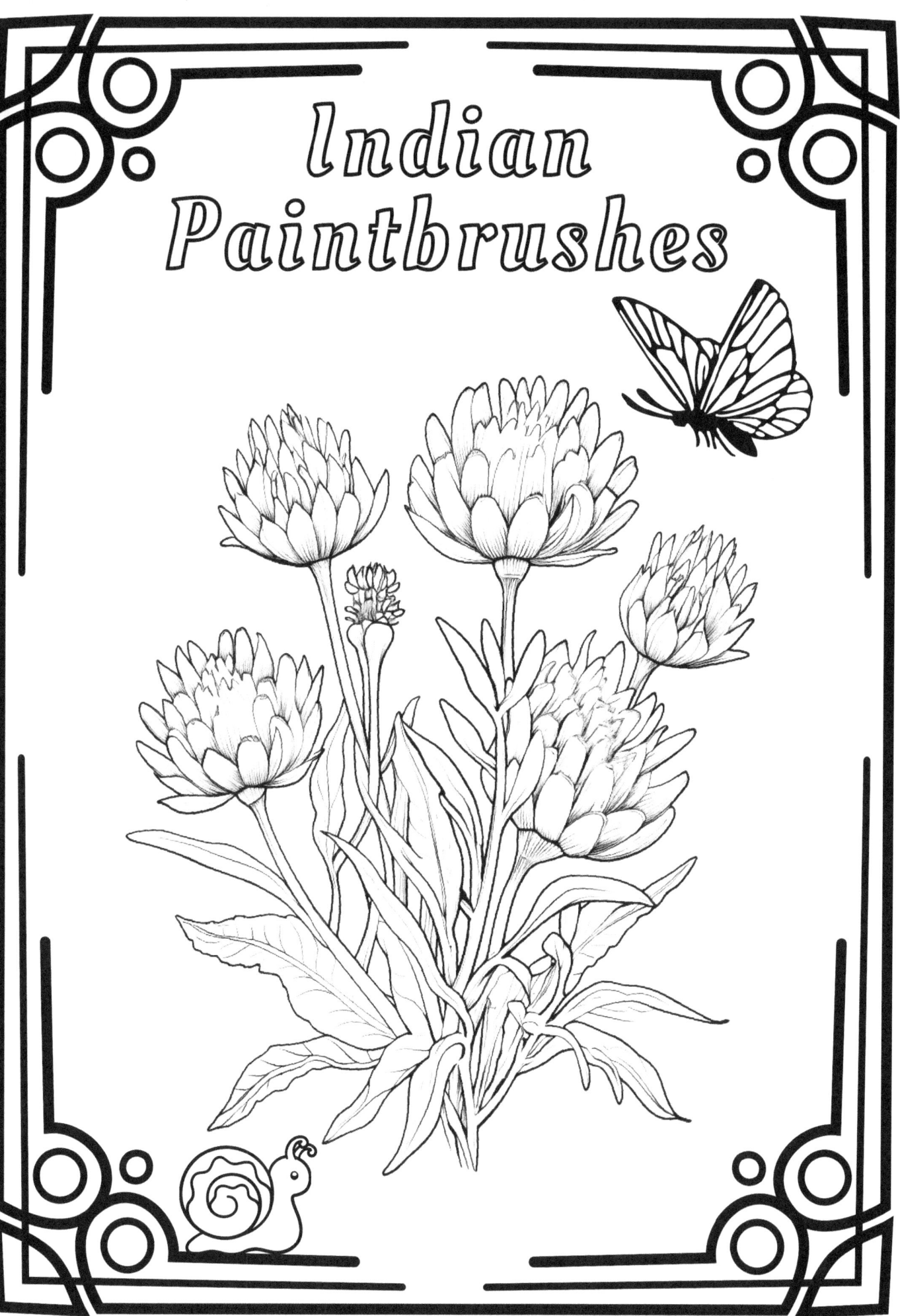

Indian Paintbrushes

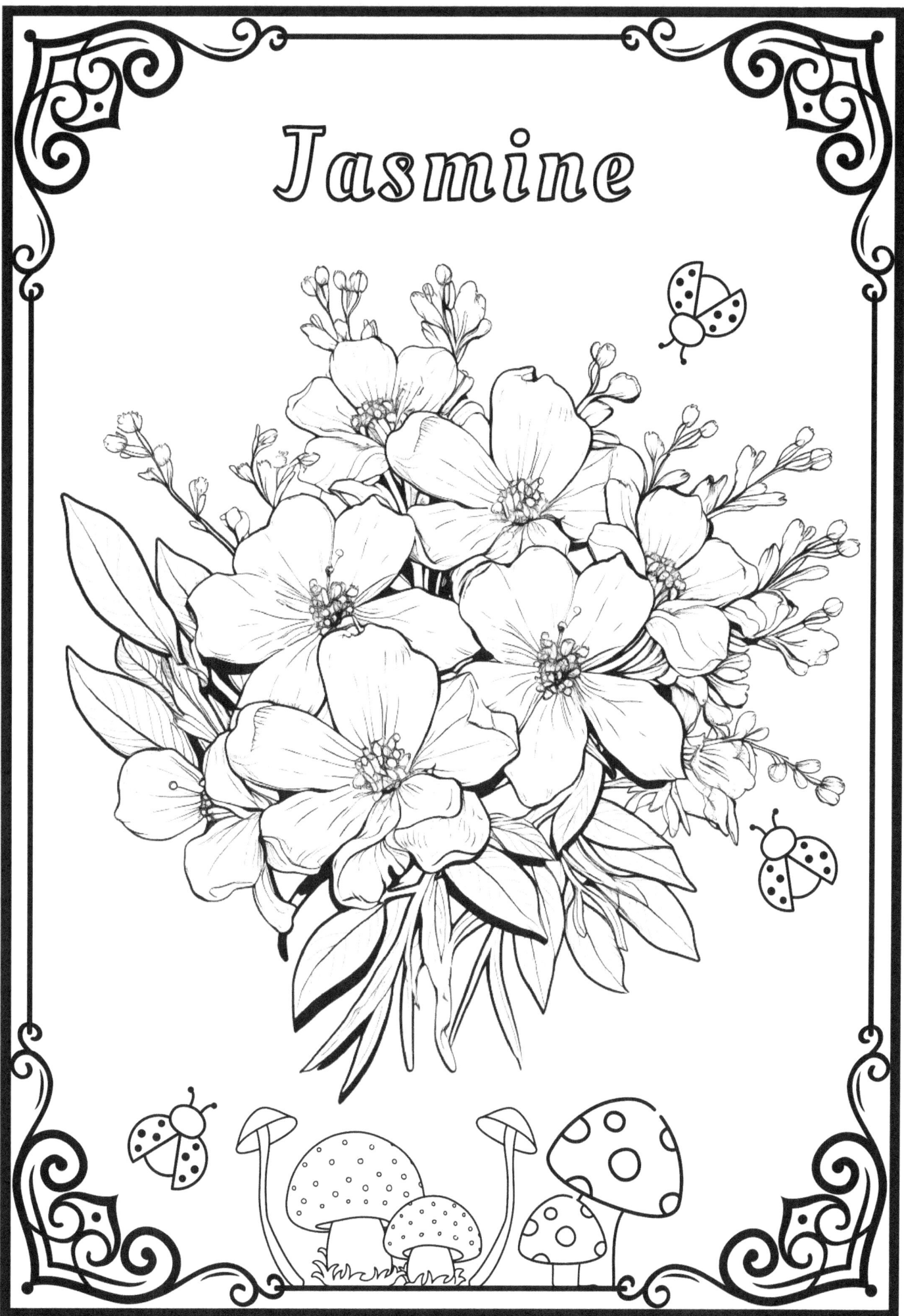

Jasmine

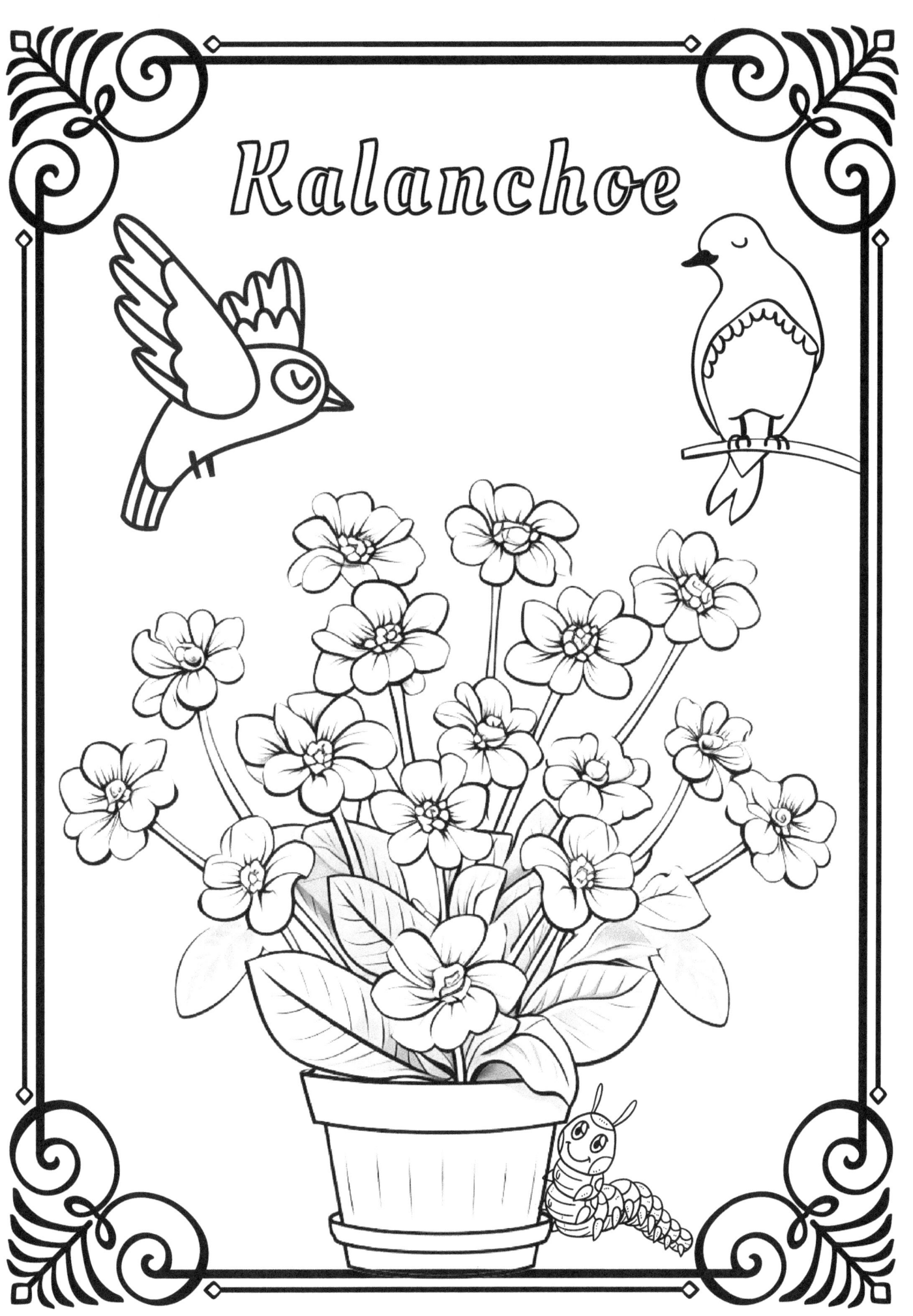

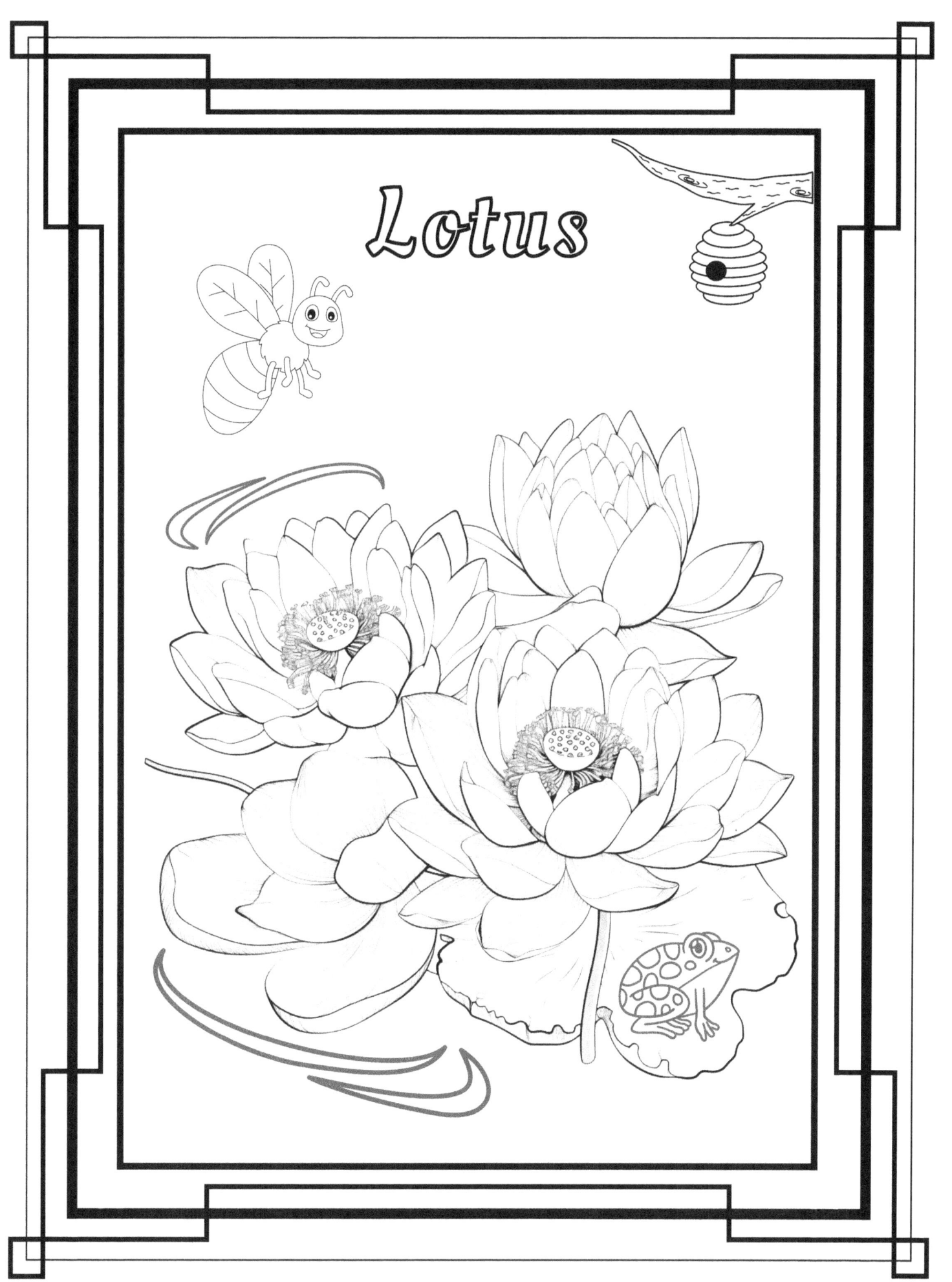

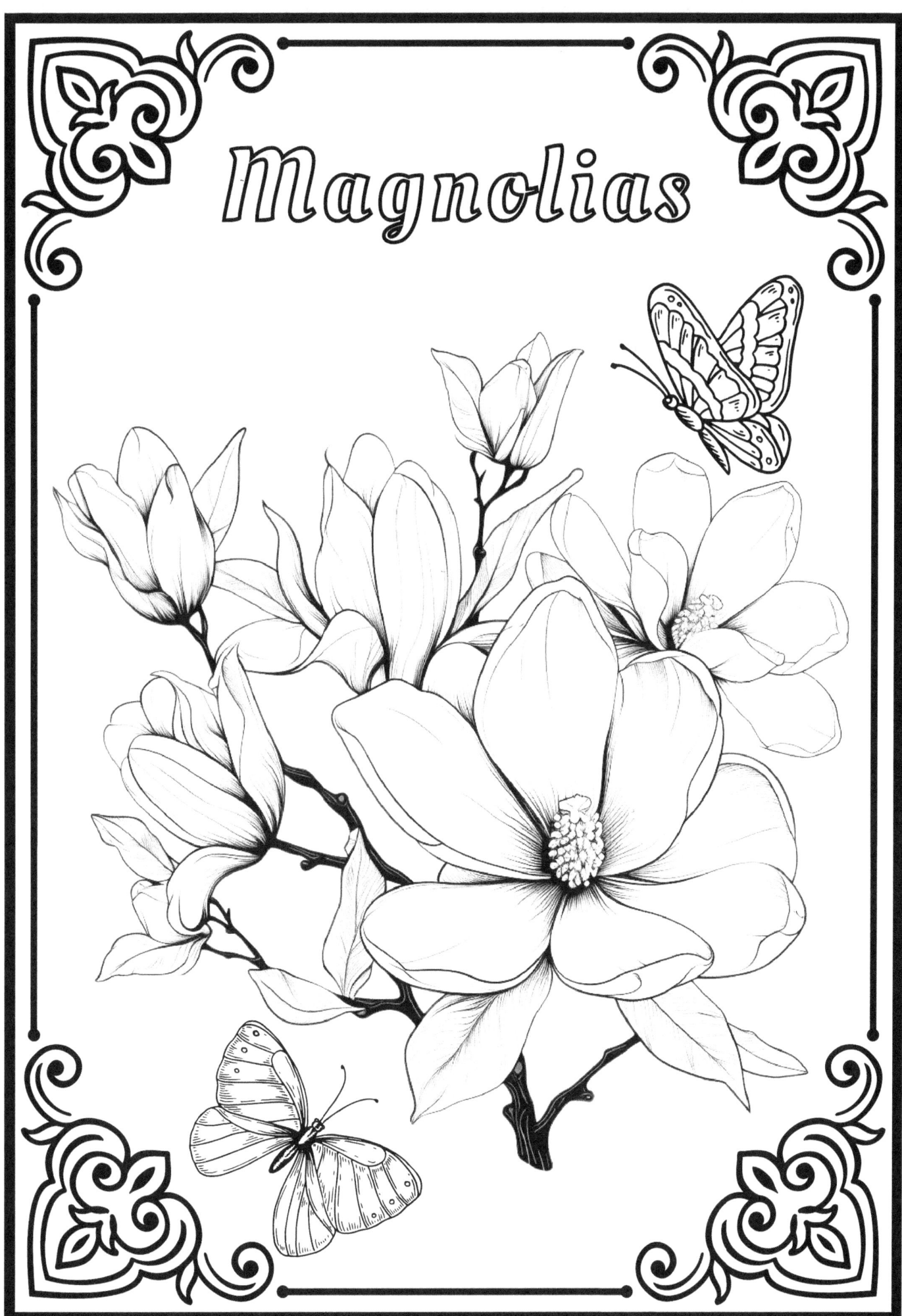

Magnolias

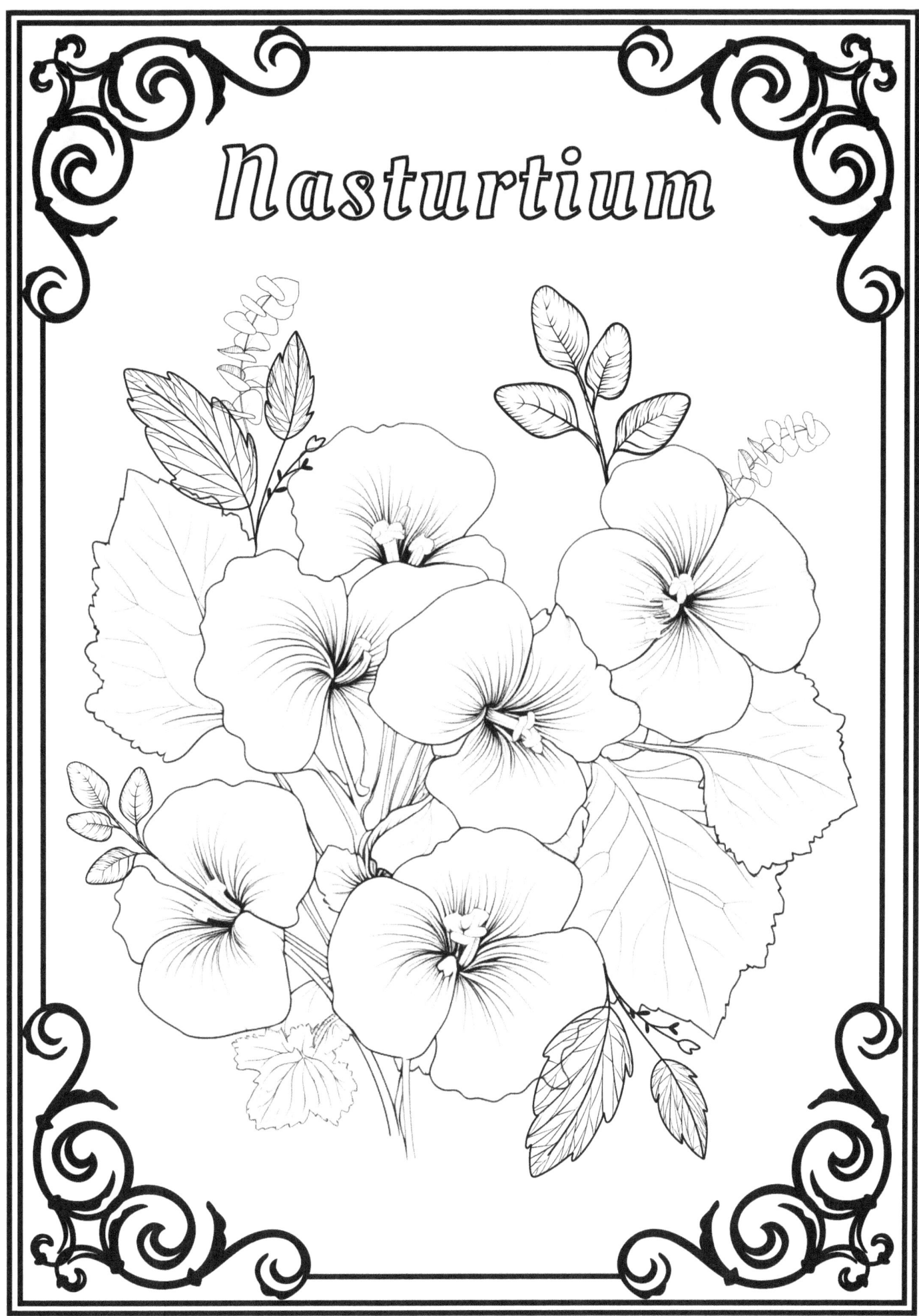

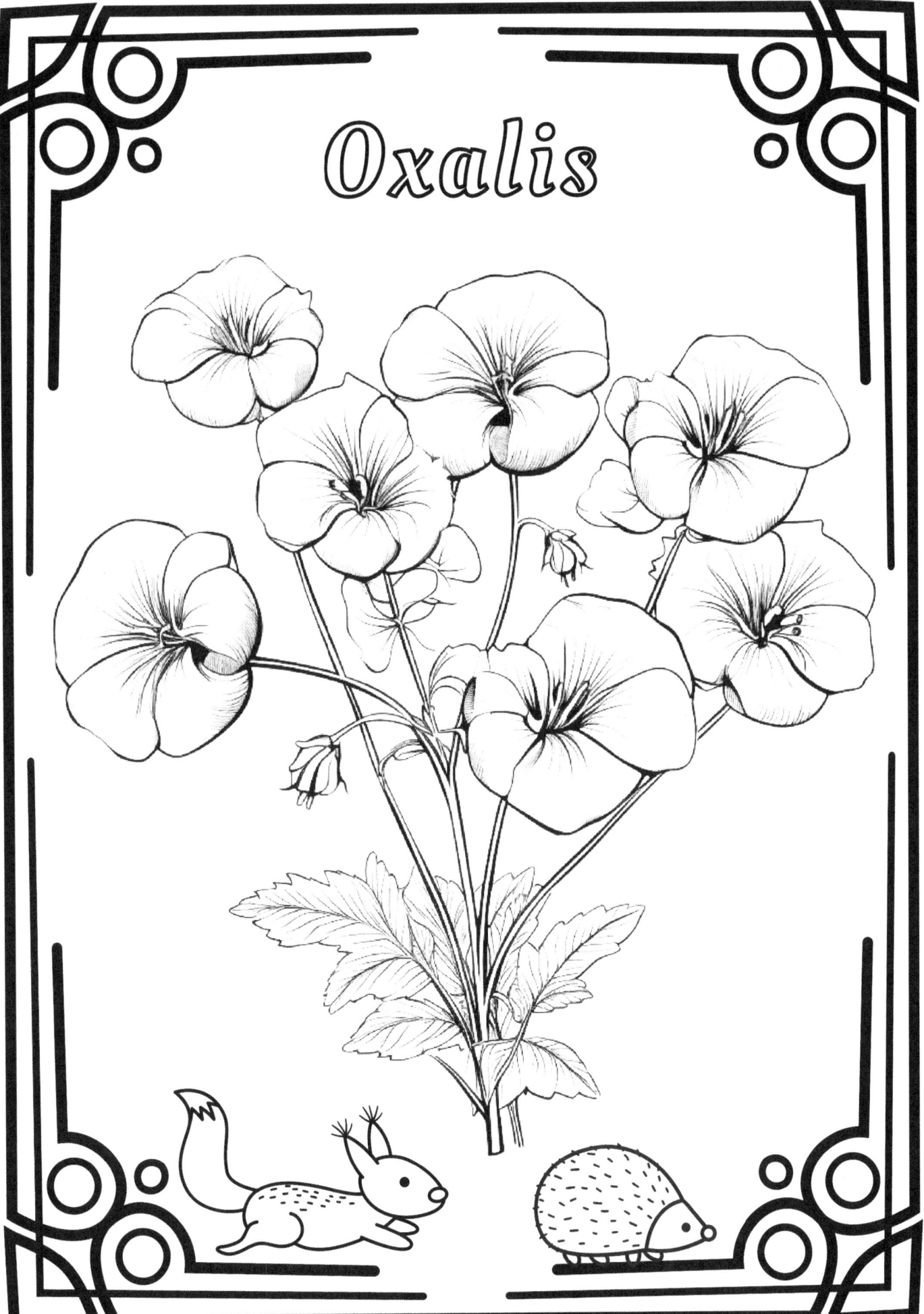

Oxalis

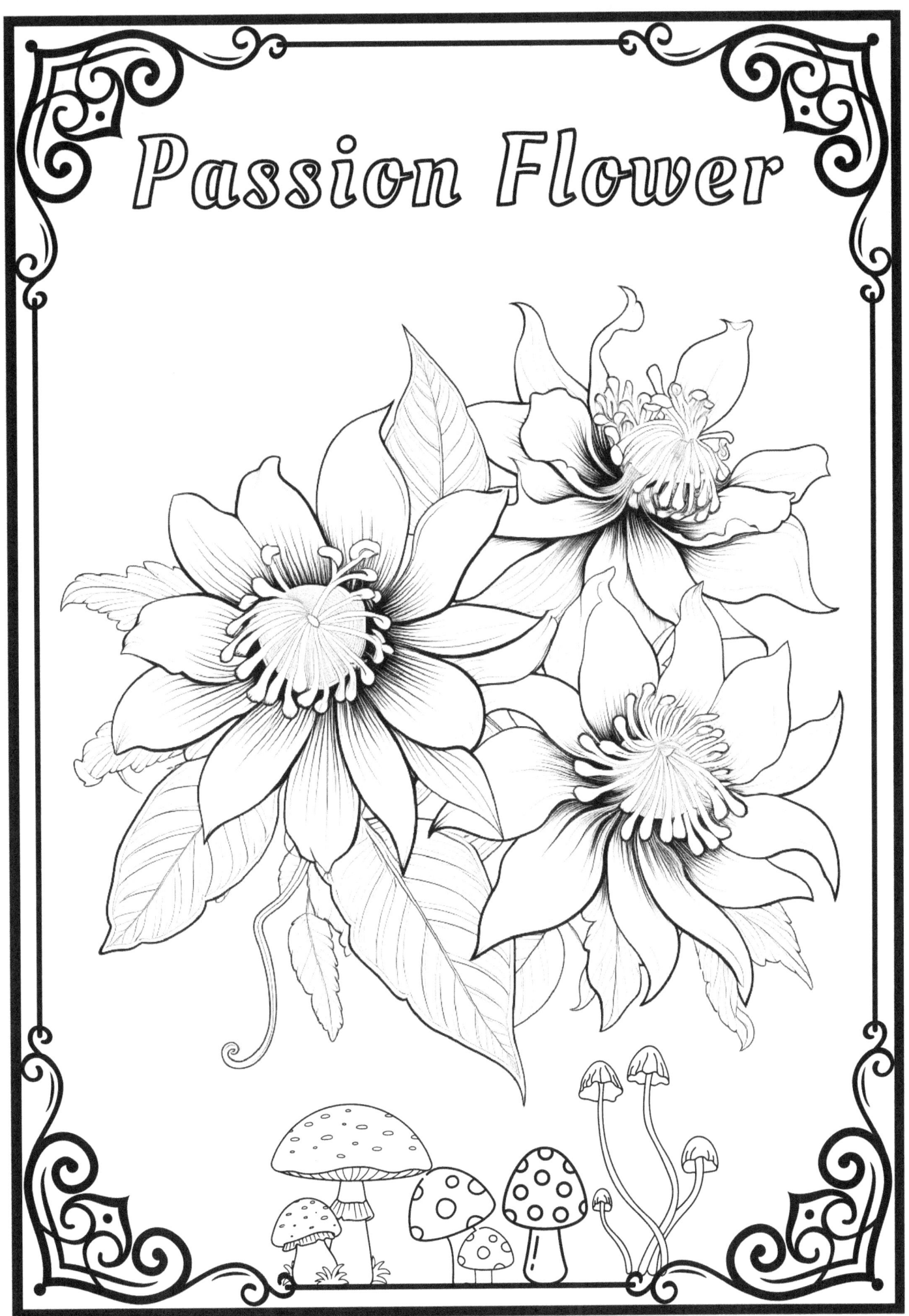

Passion Flower

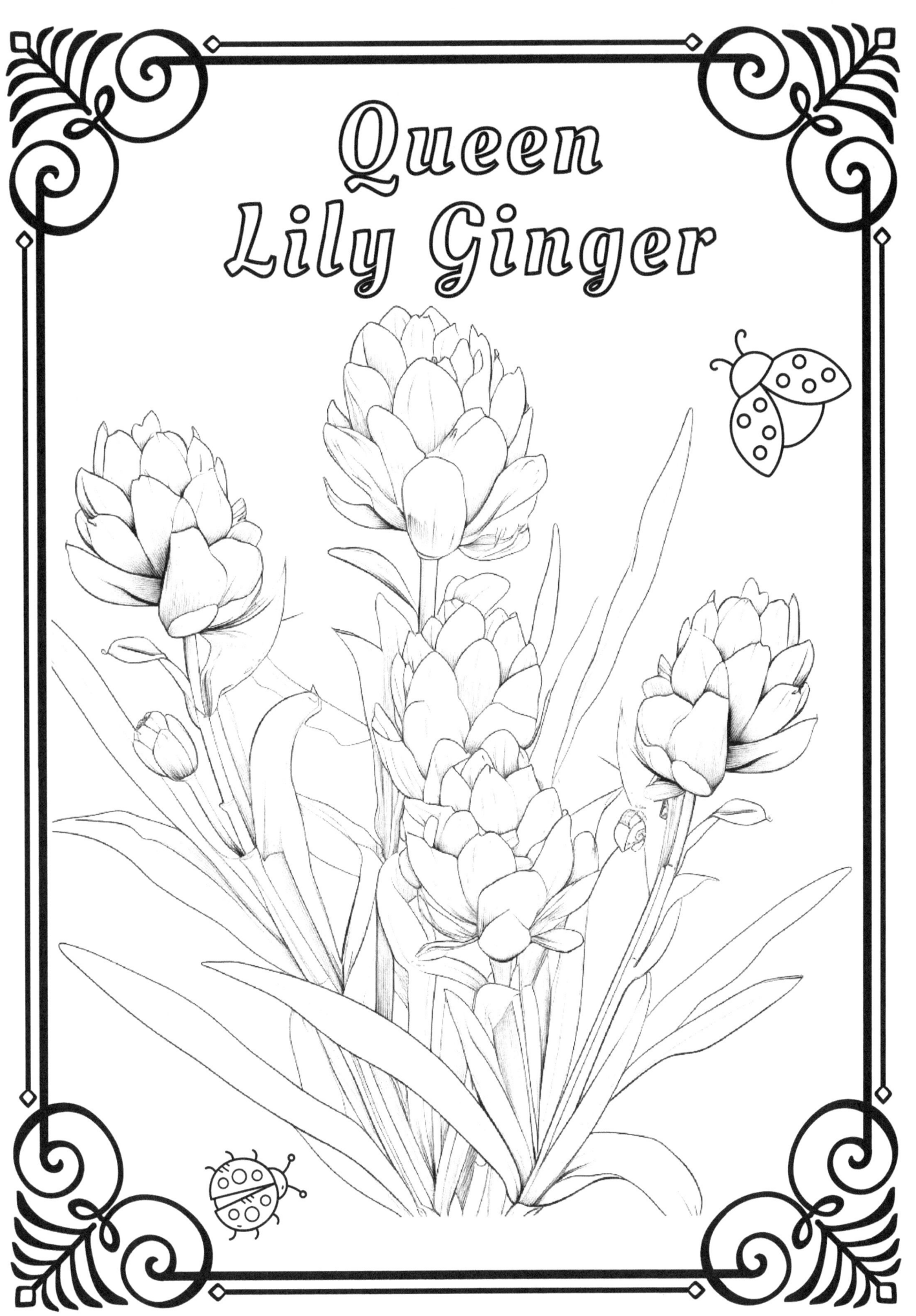

Queen
Lily Ginger

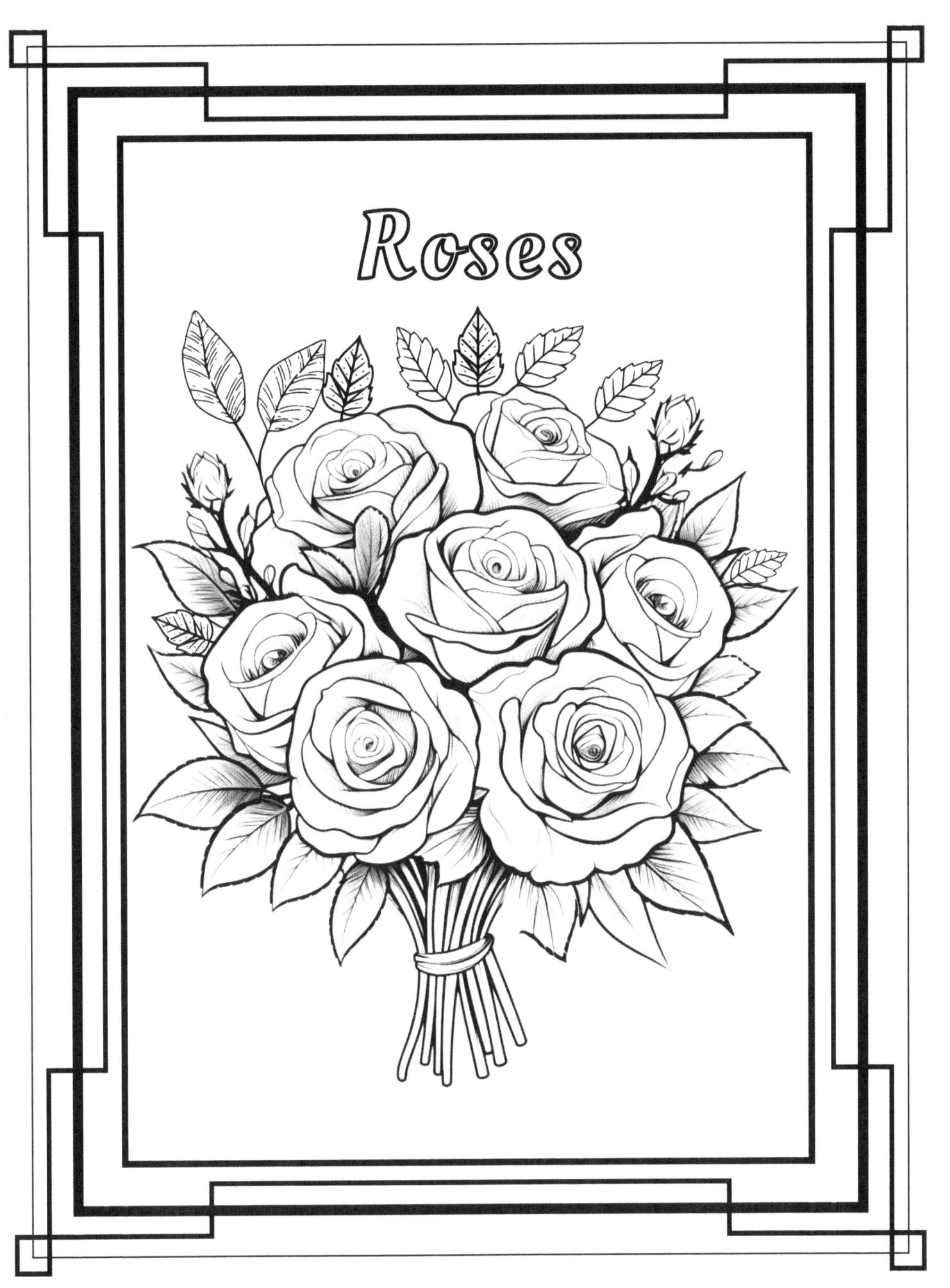

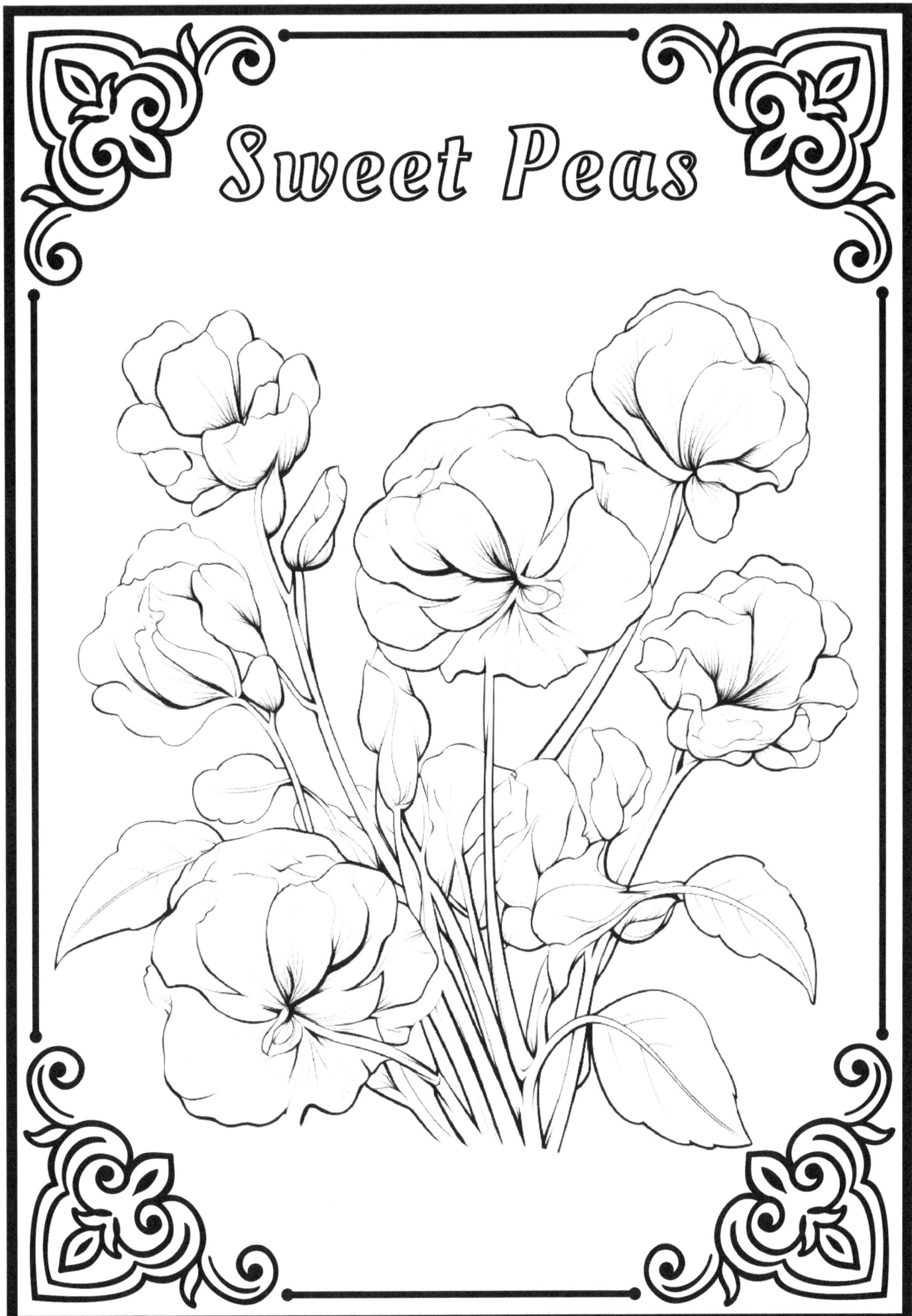

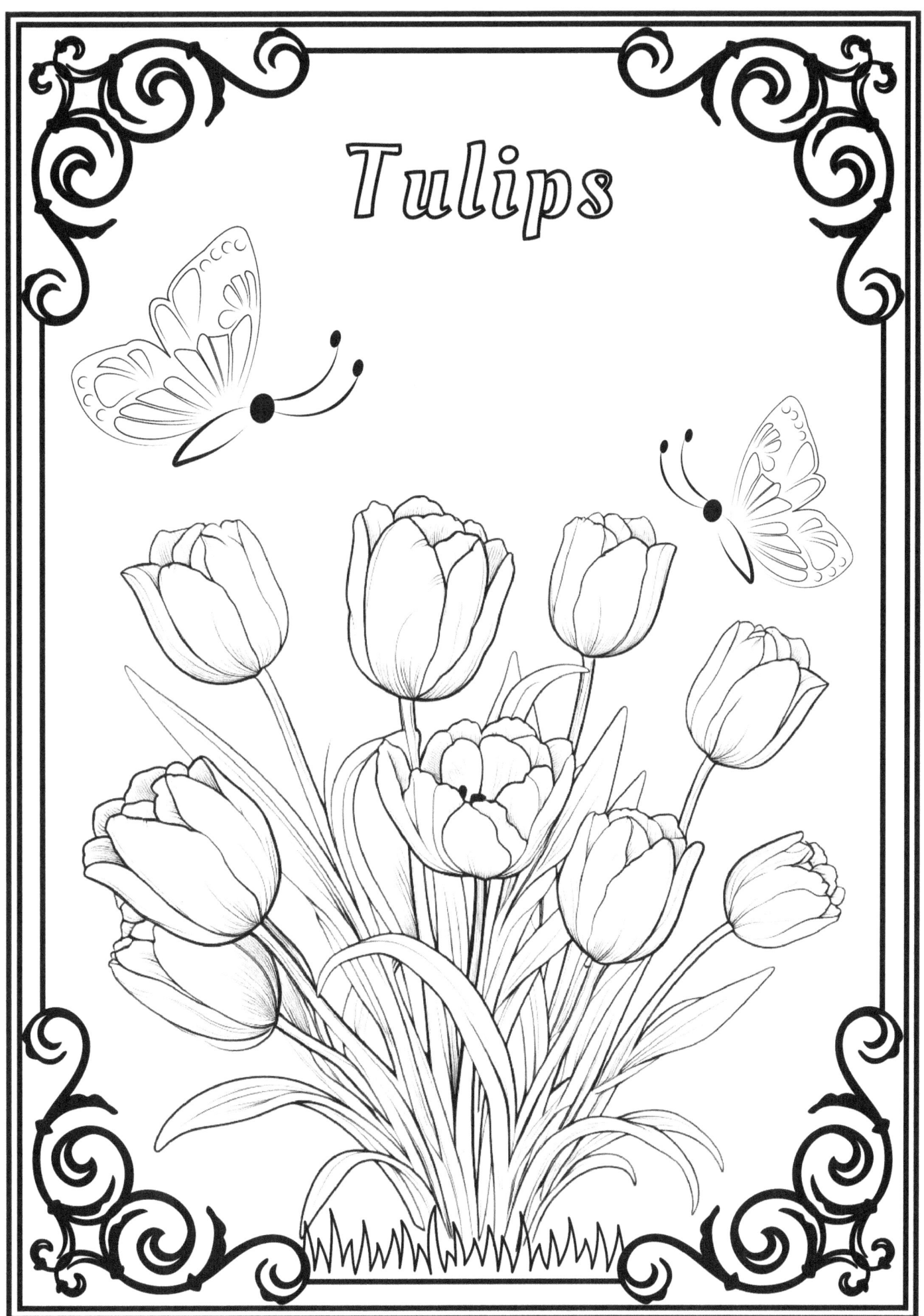

Tulips

Umbrella Plant

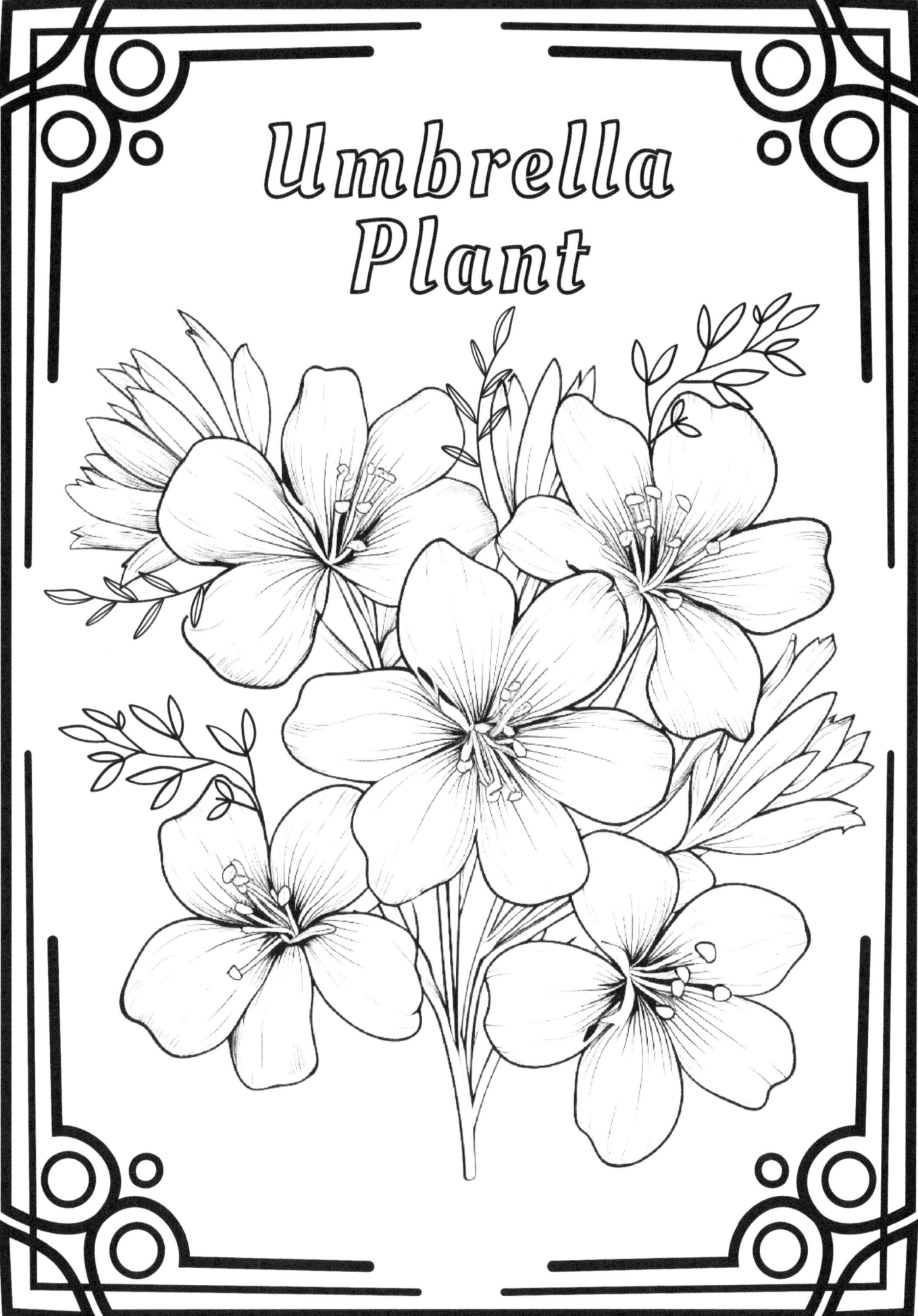

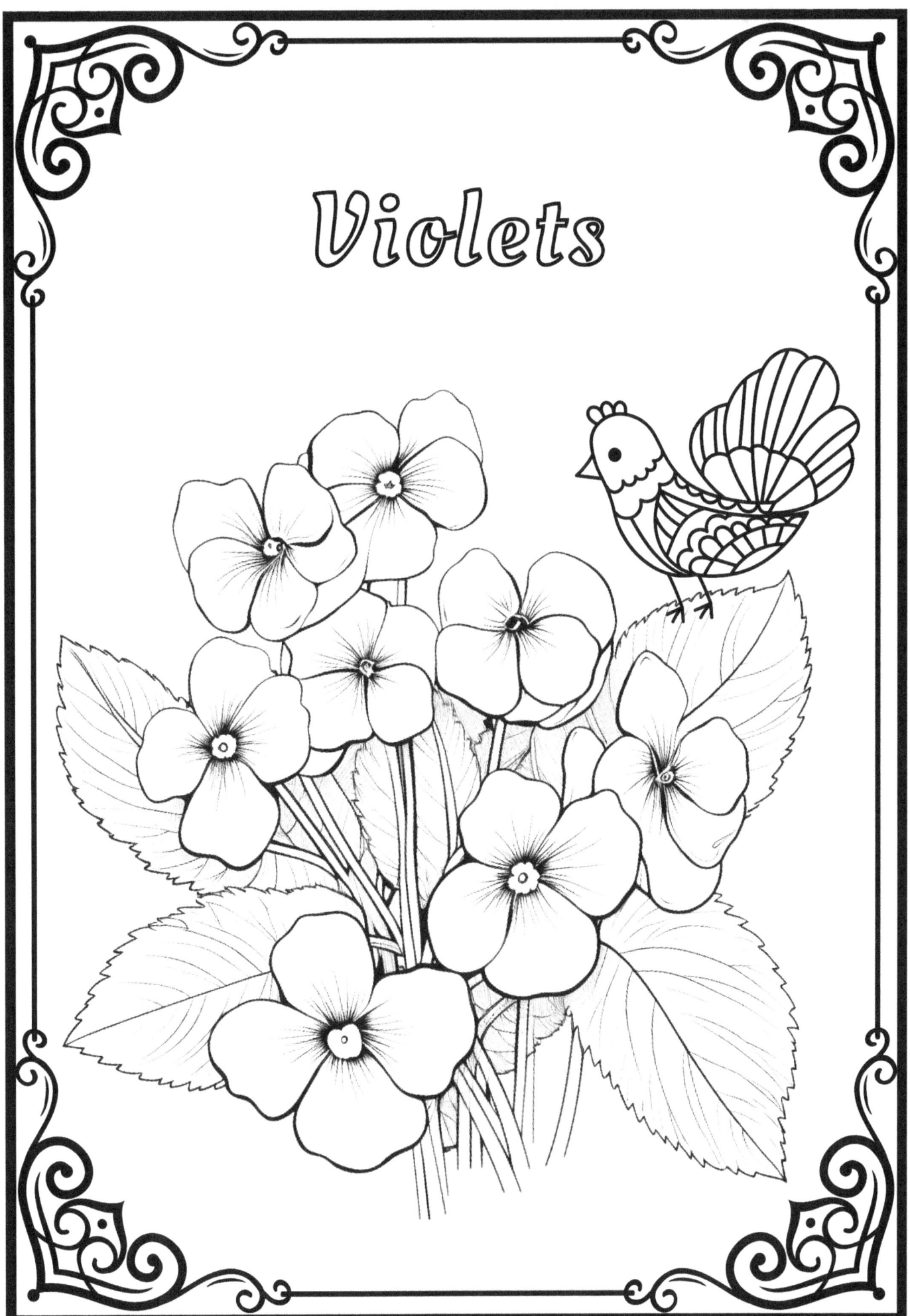

Wisteria

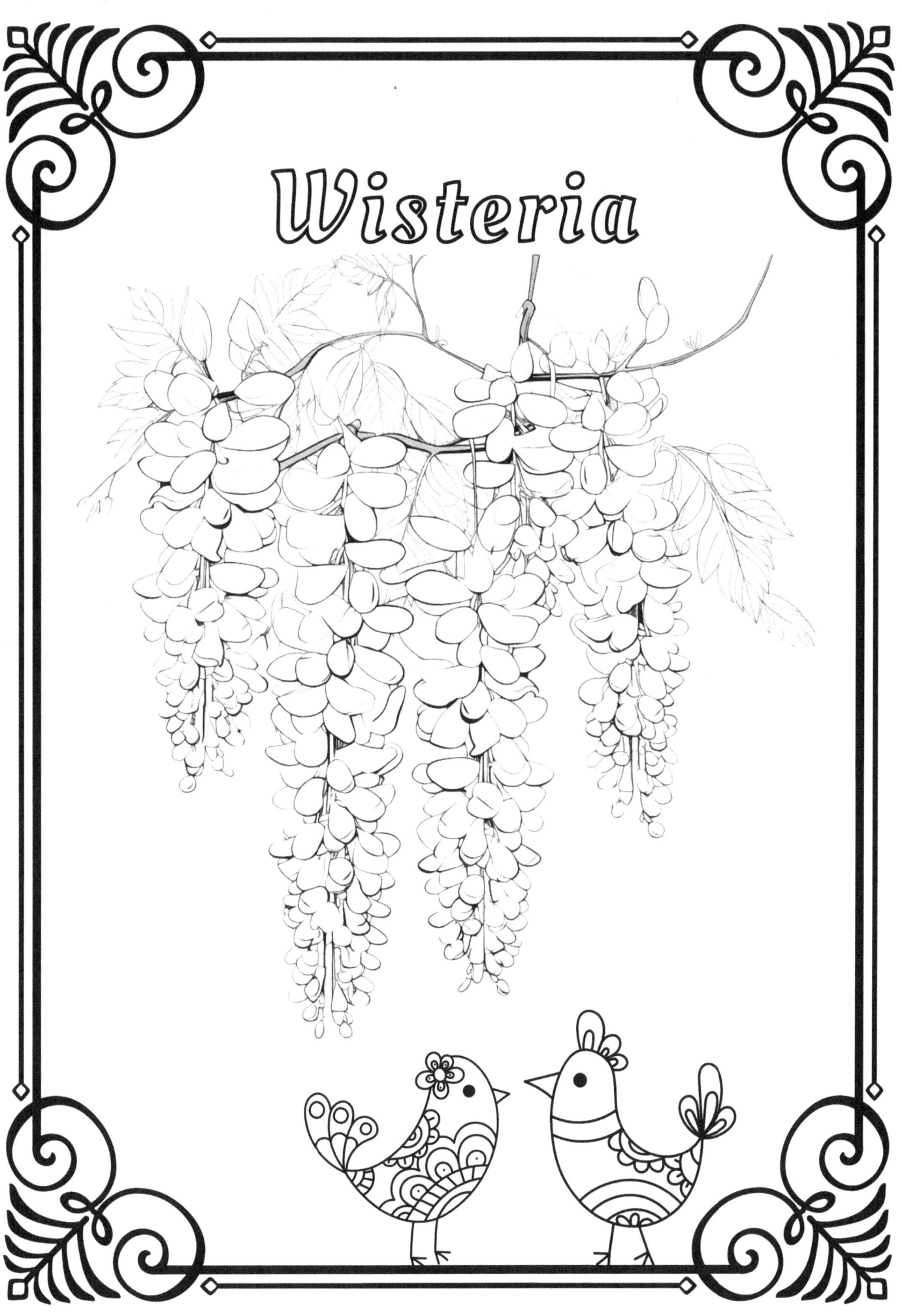

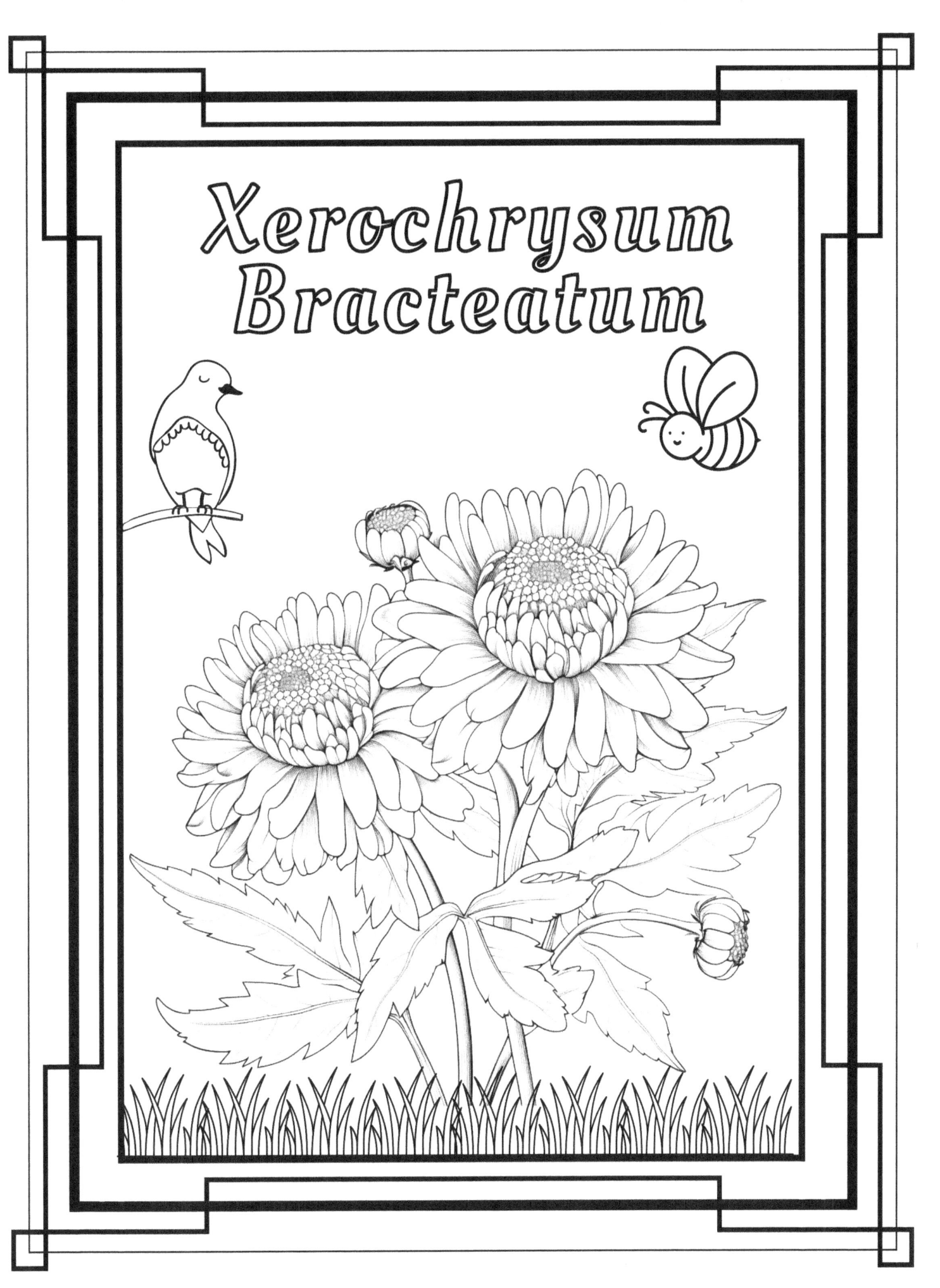

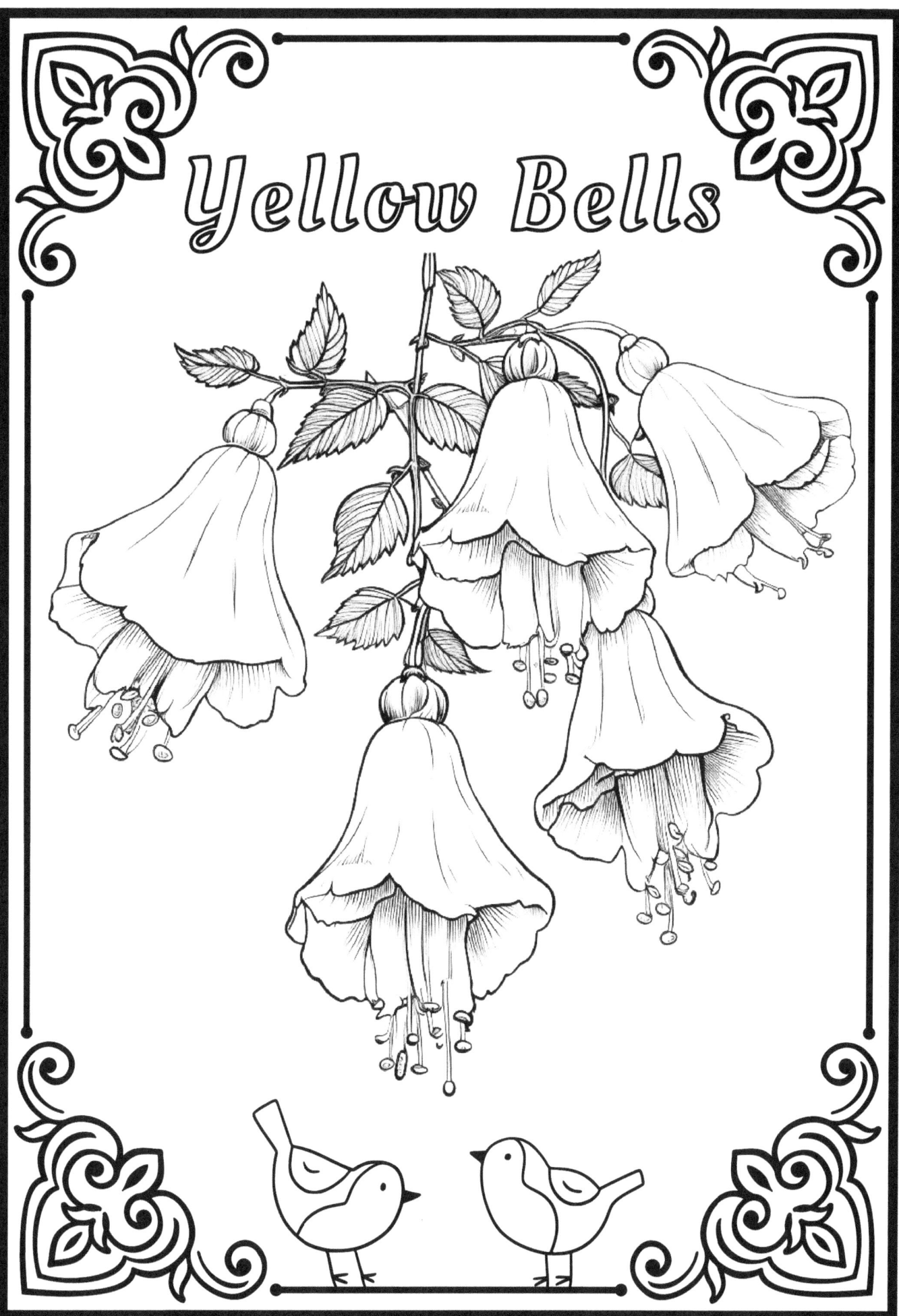

Yellow Bells

Zinnias

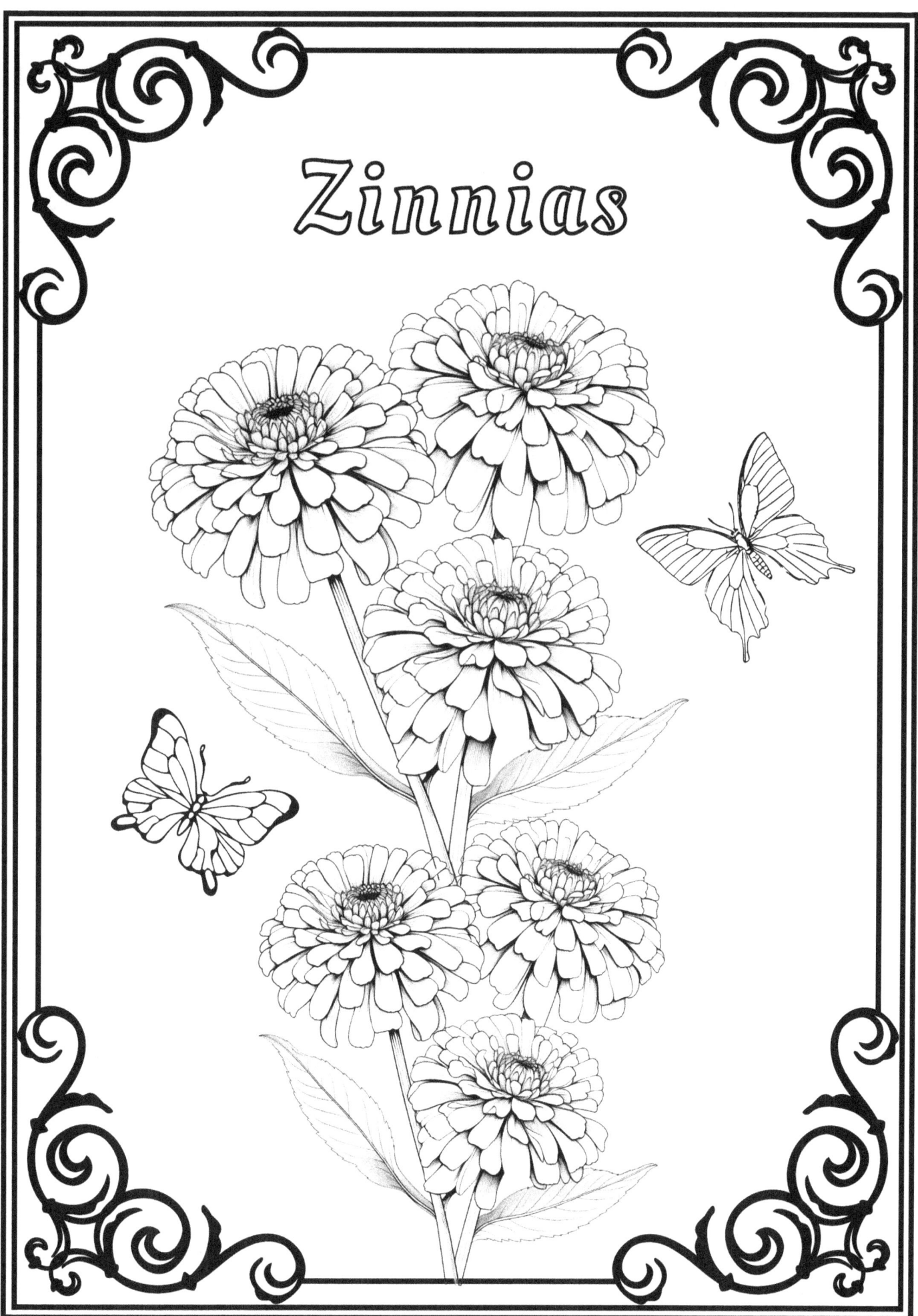

Bonus Content

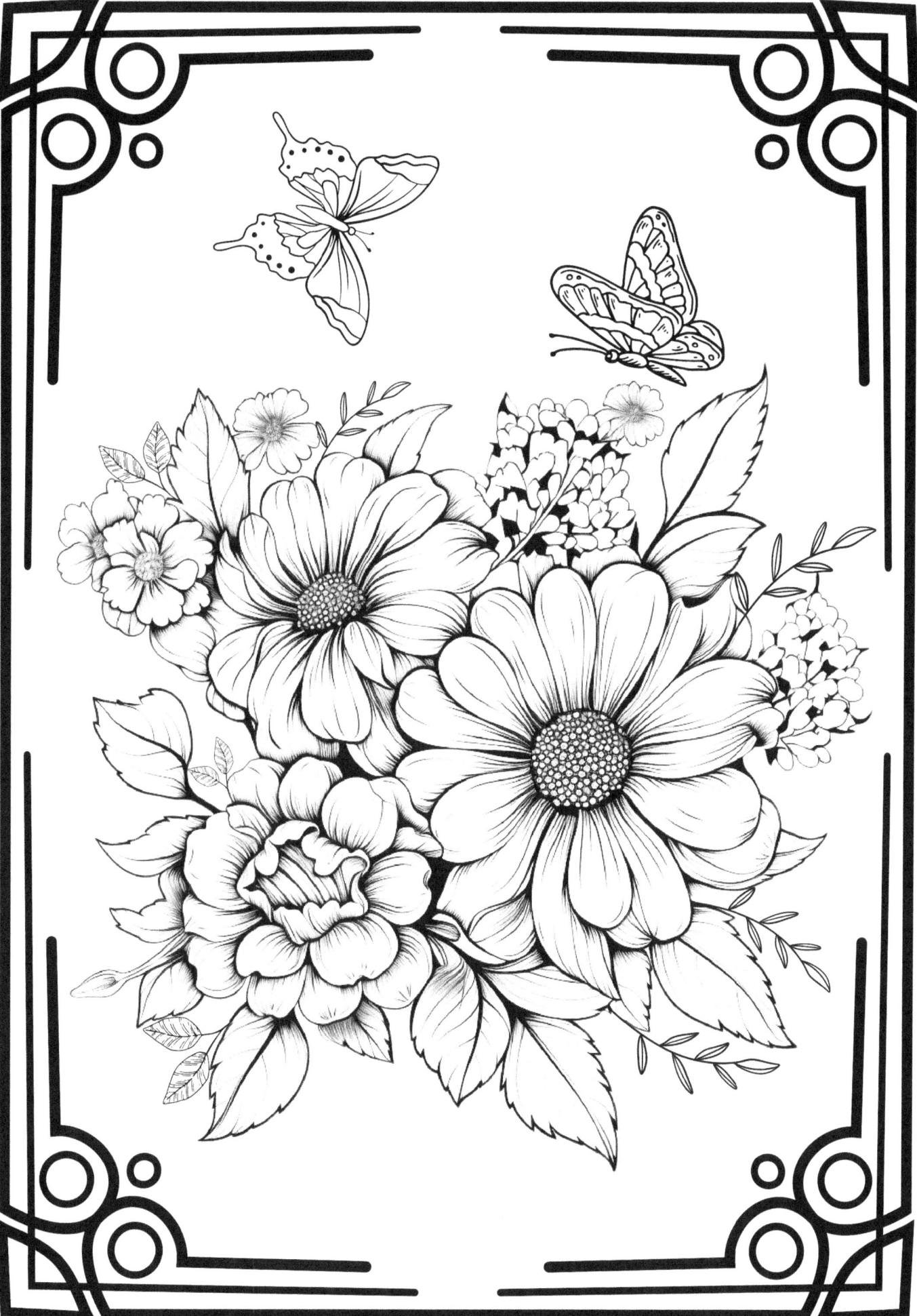

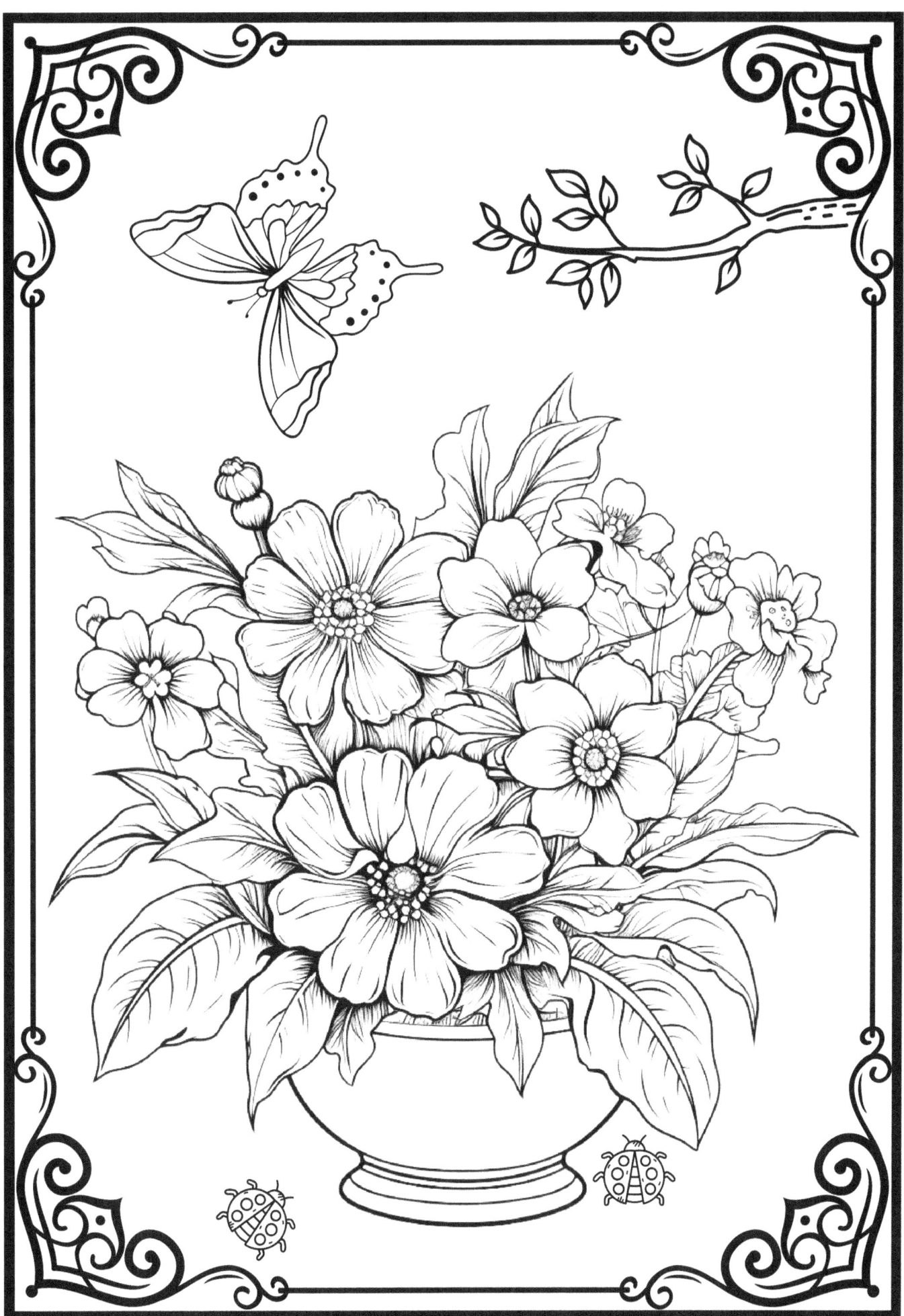

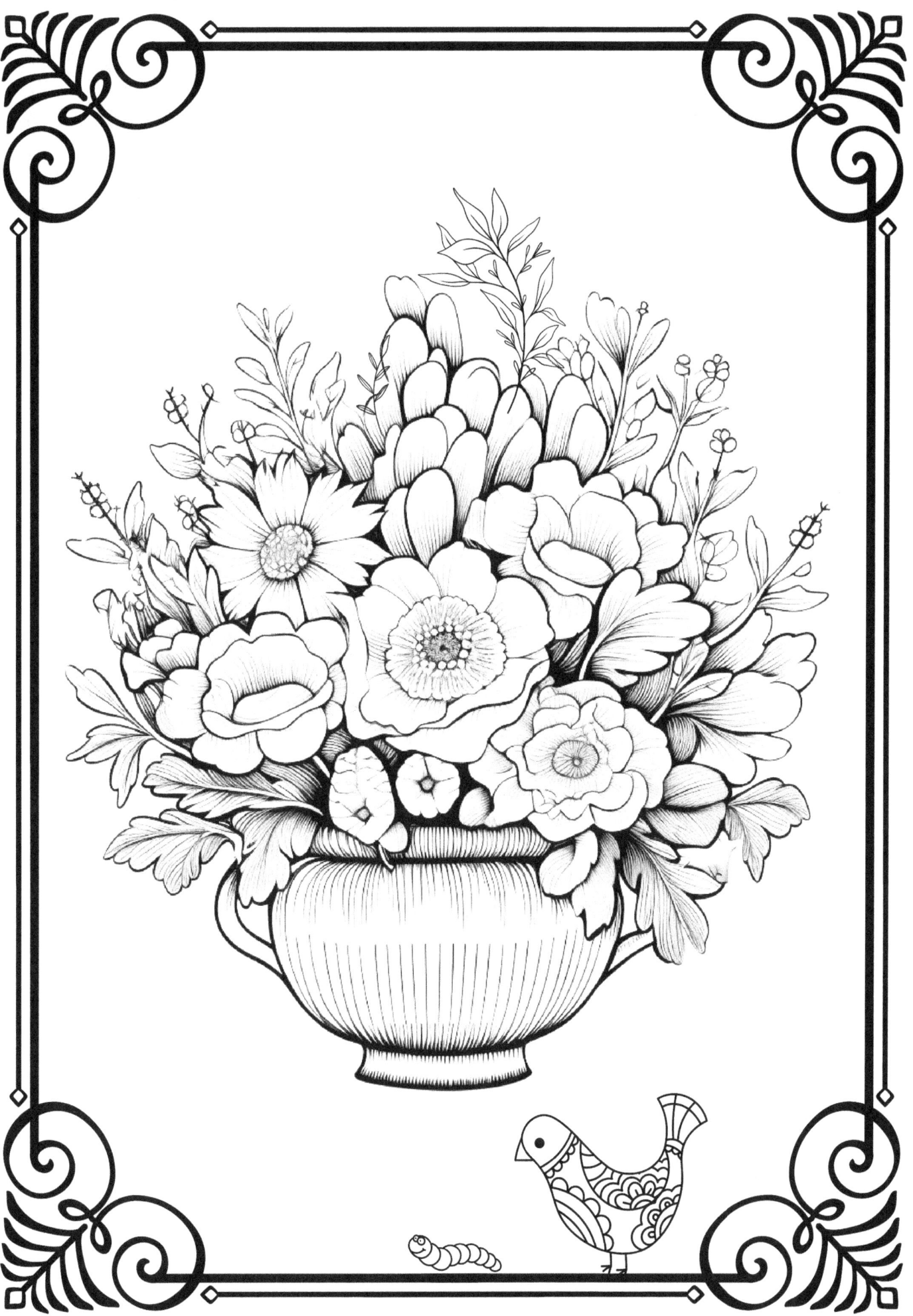

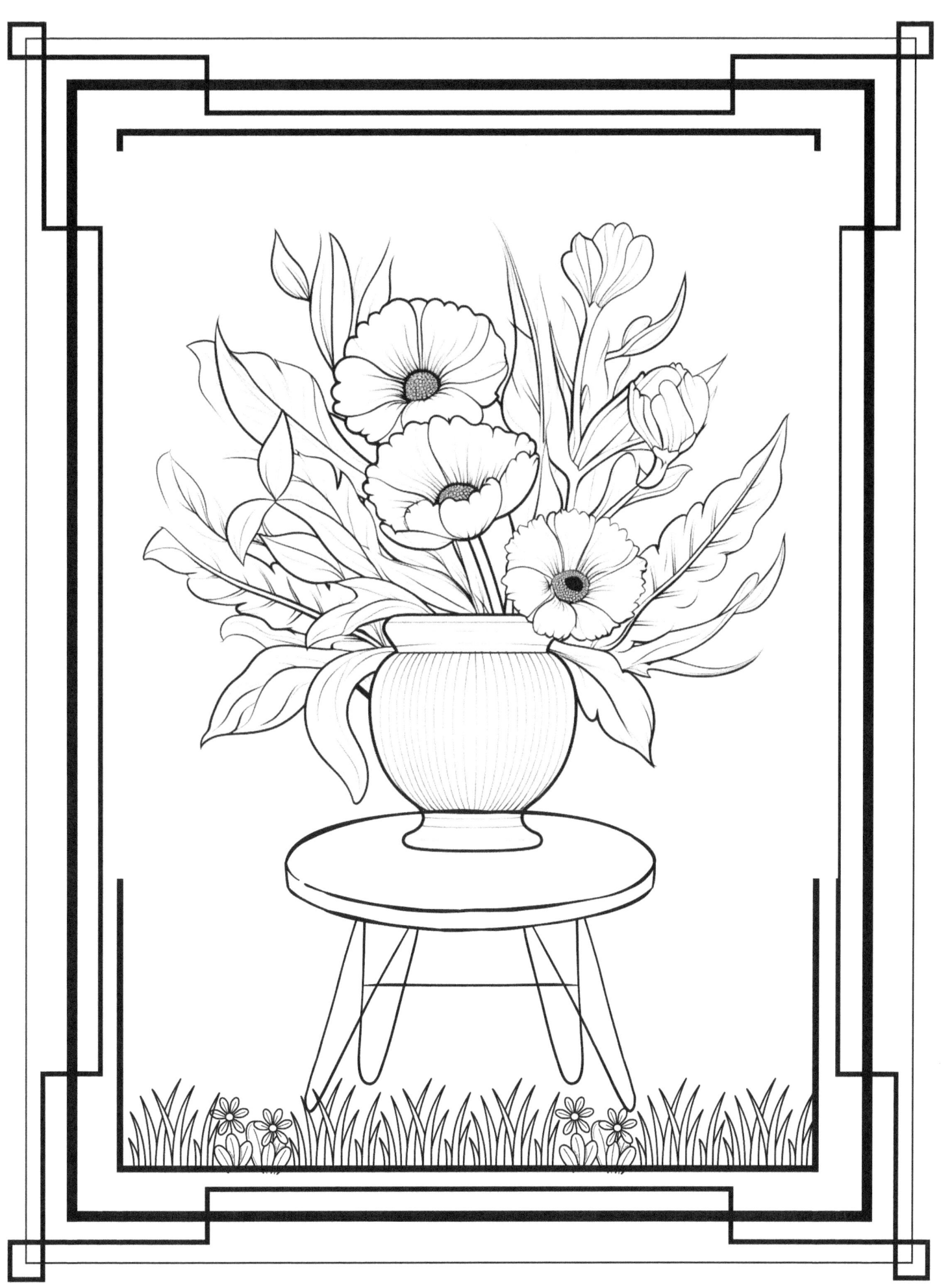

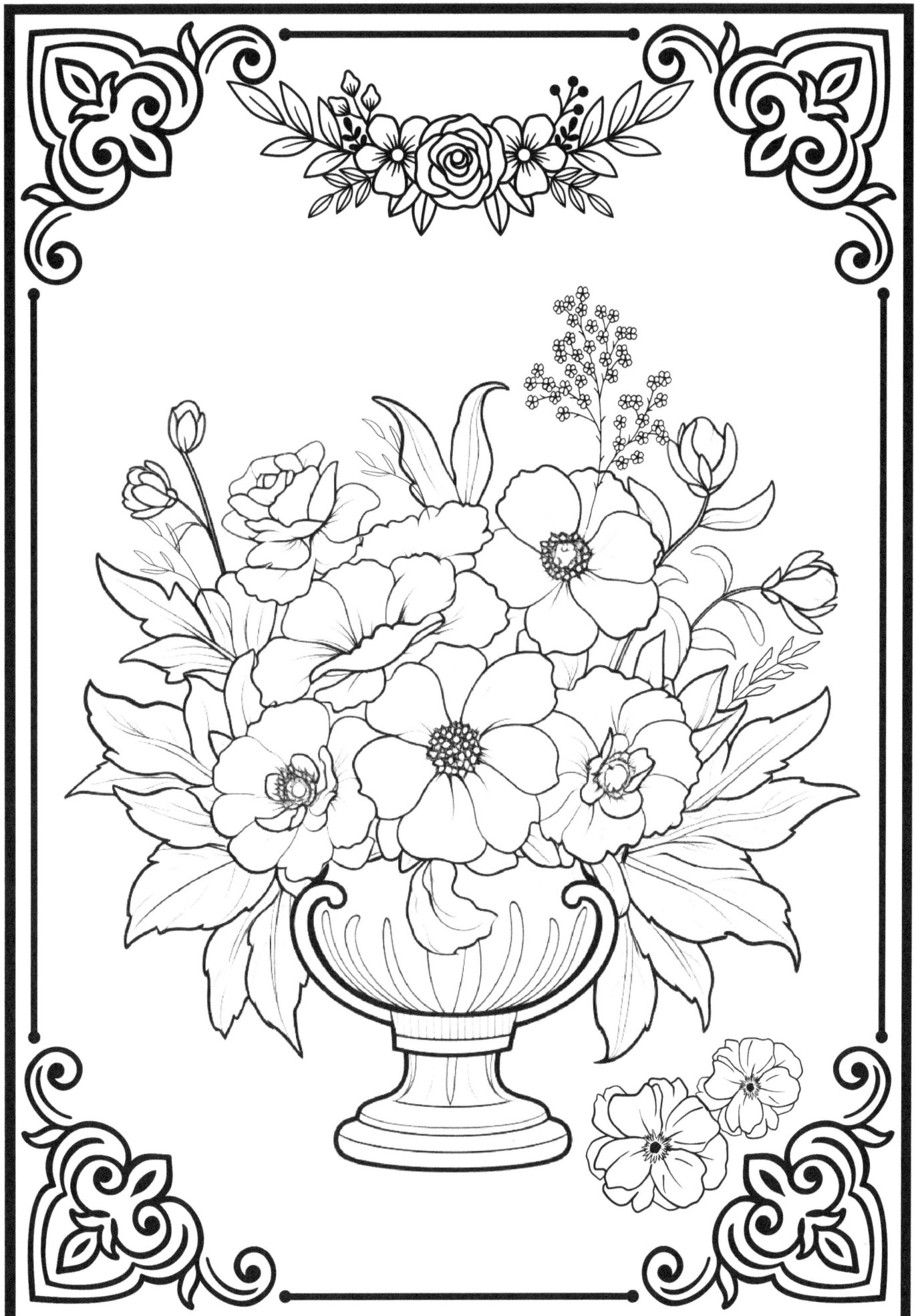

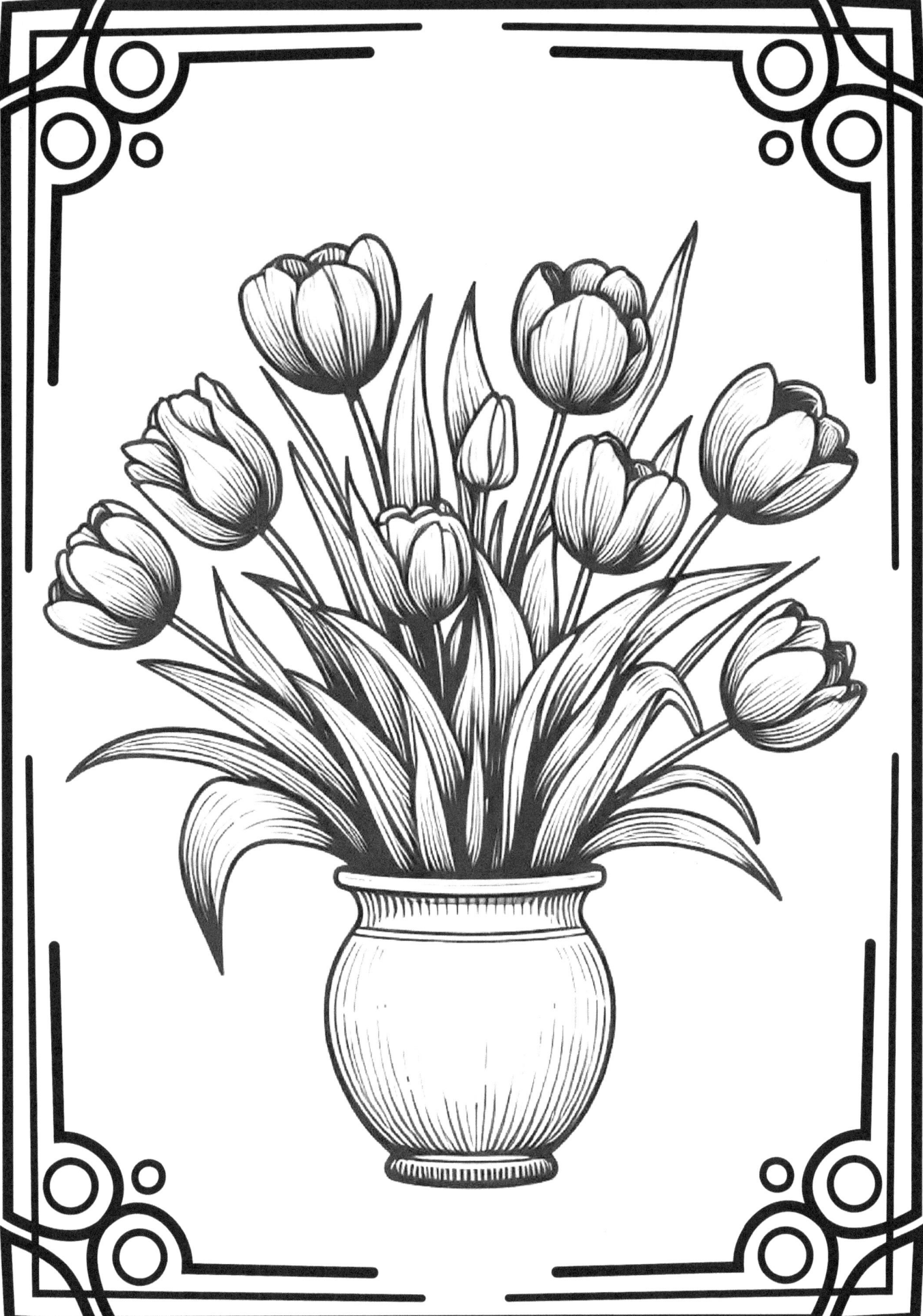

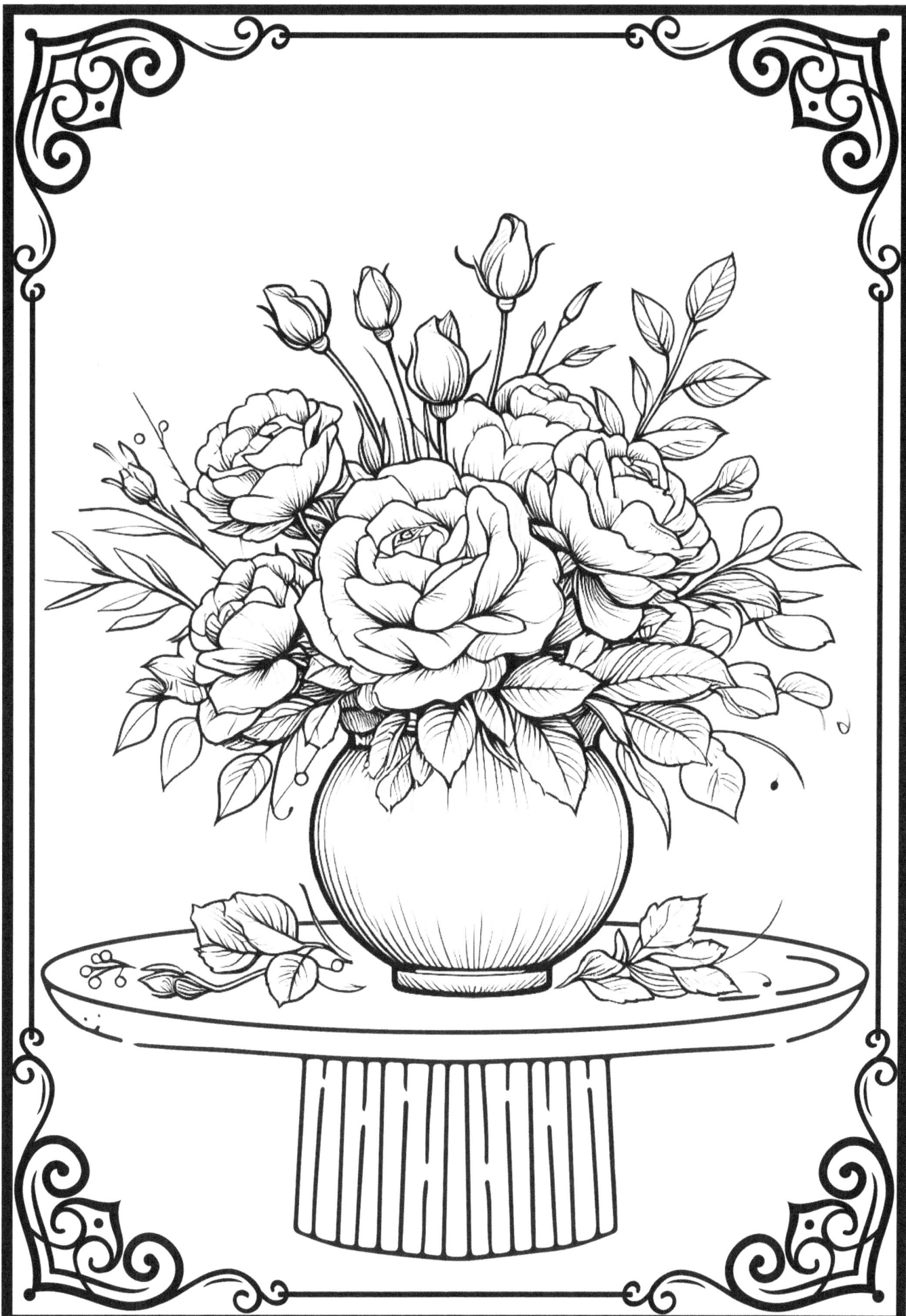

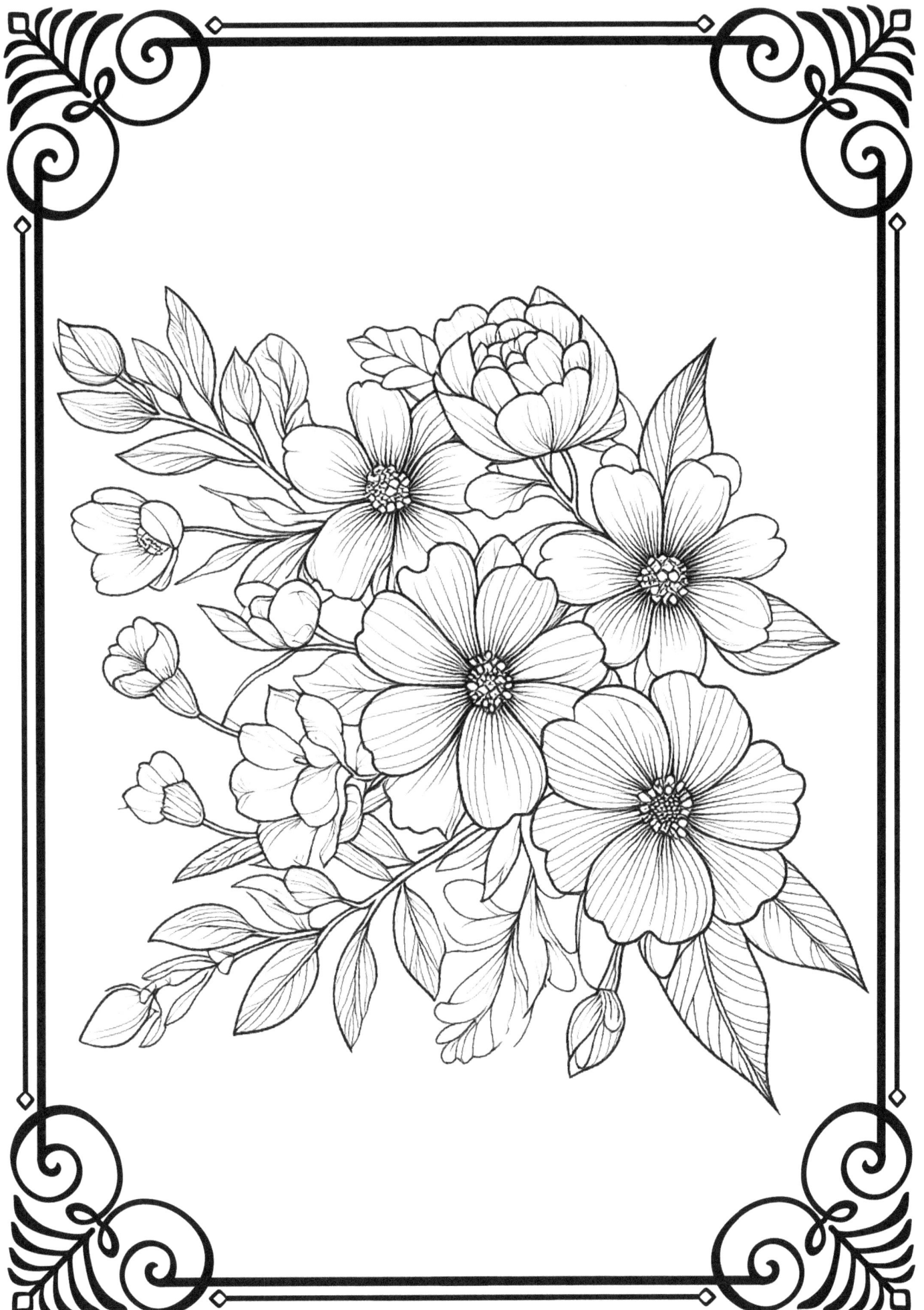

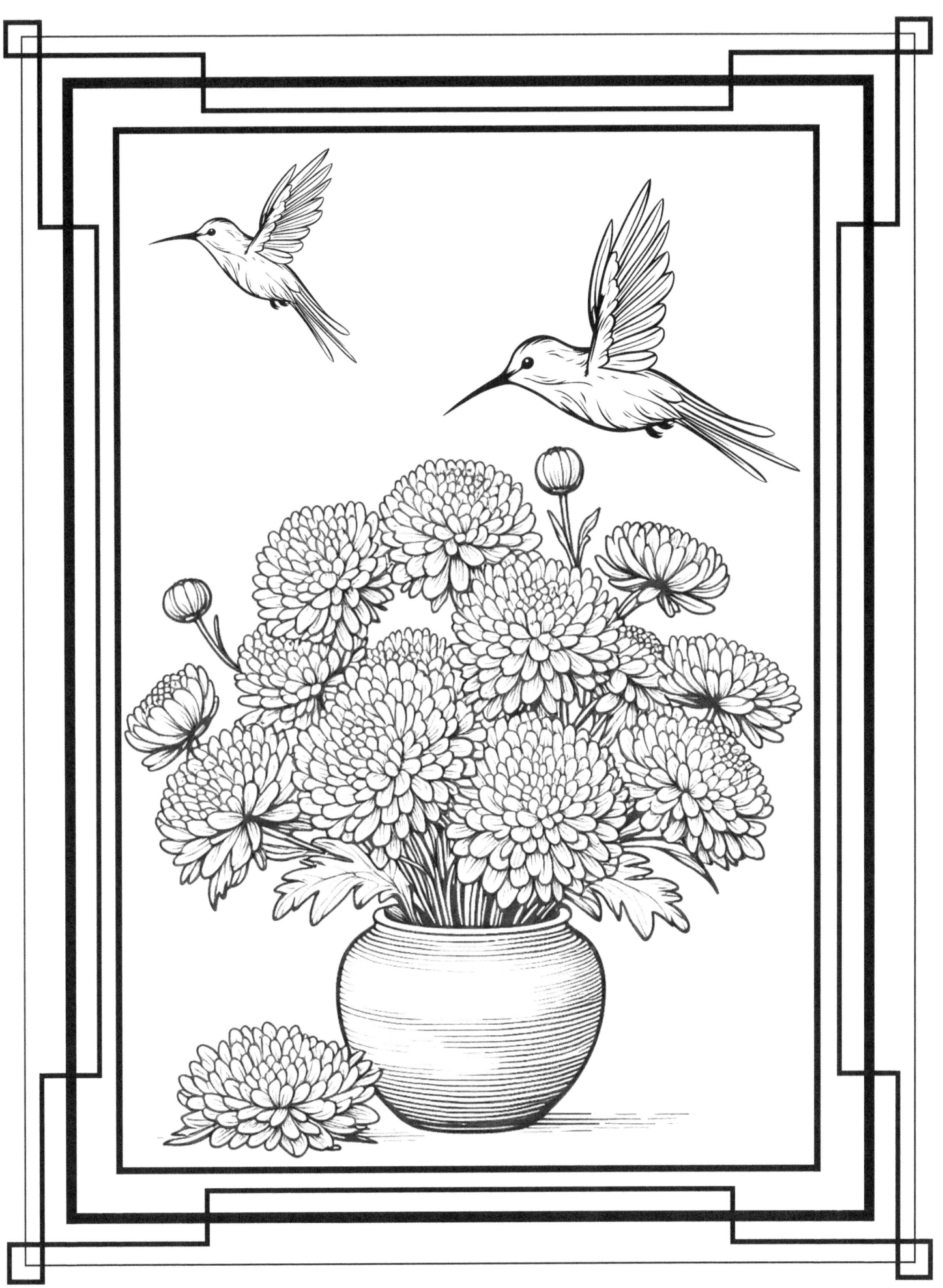

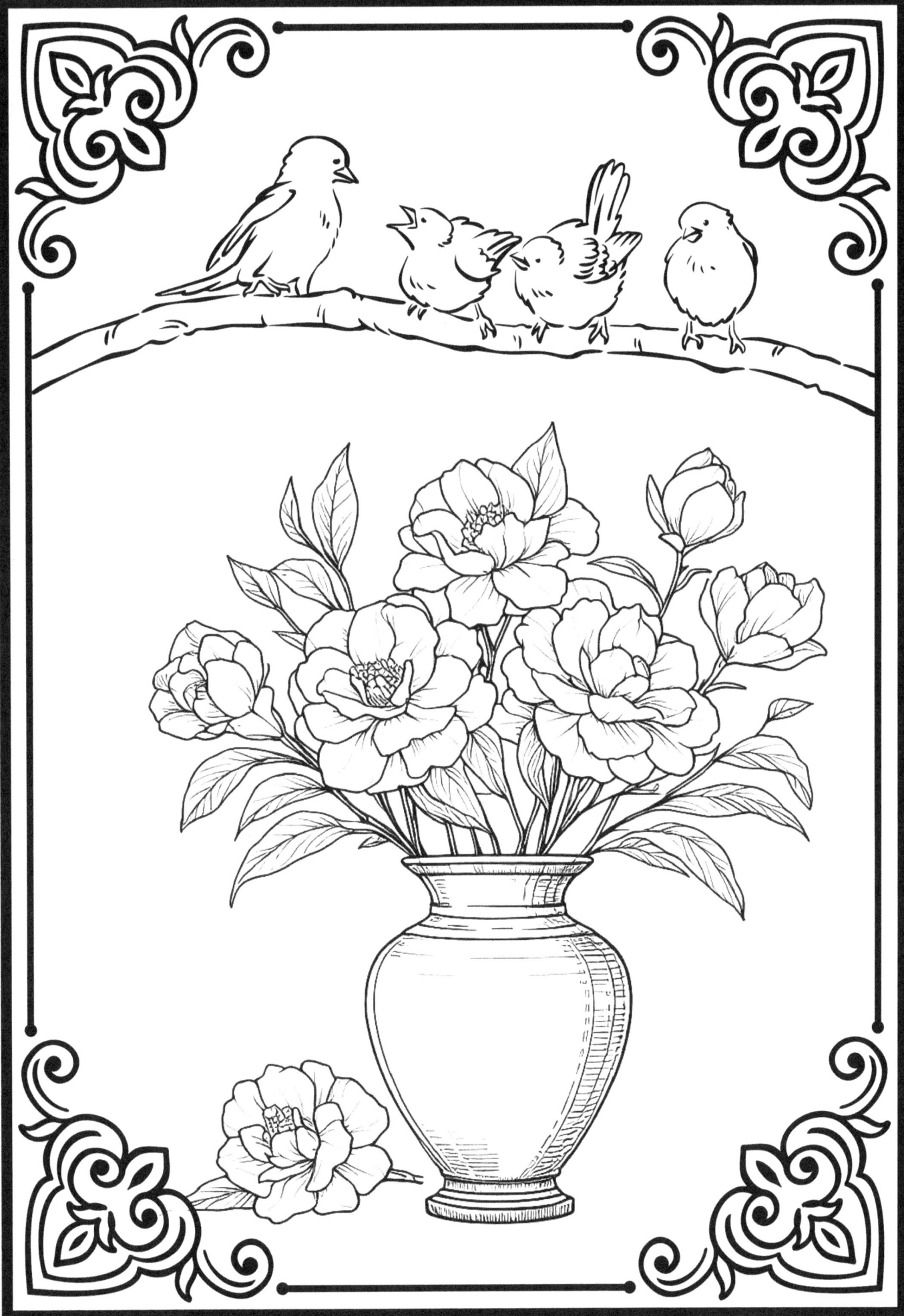

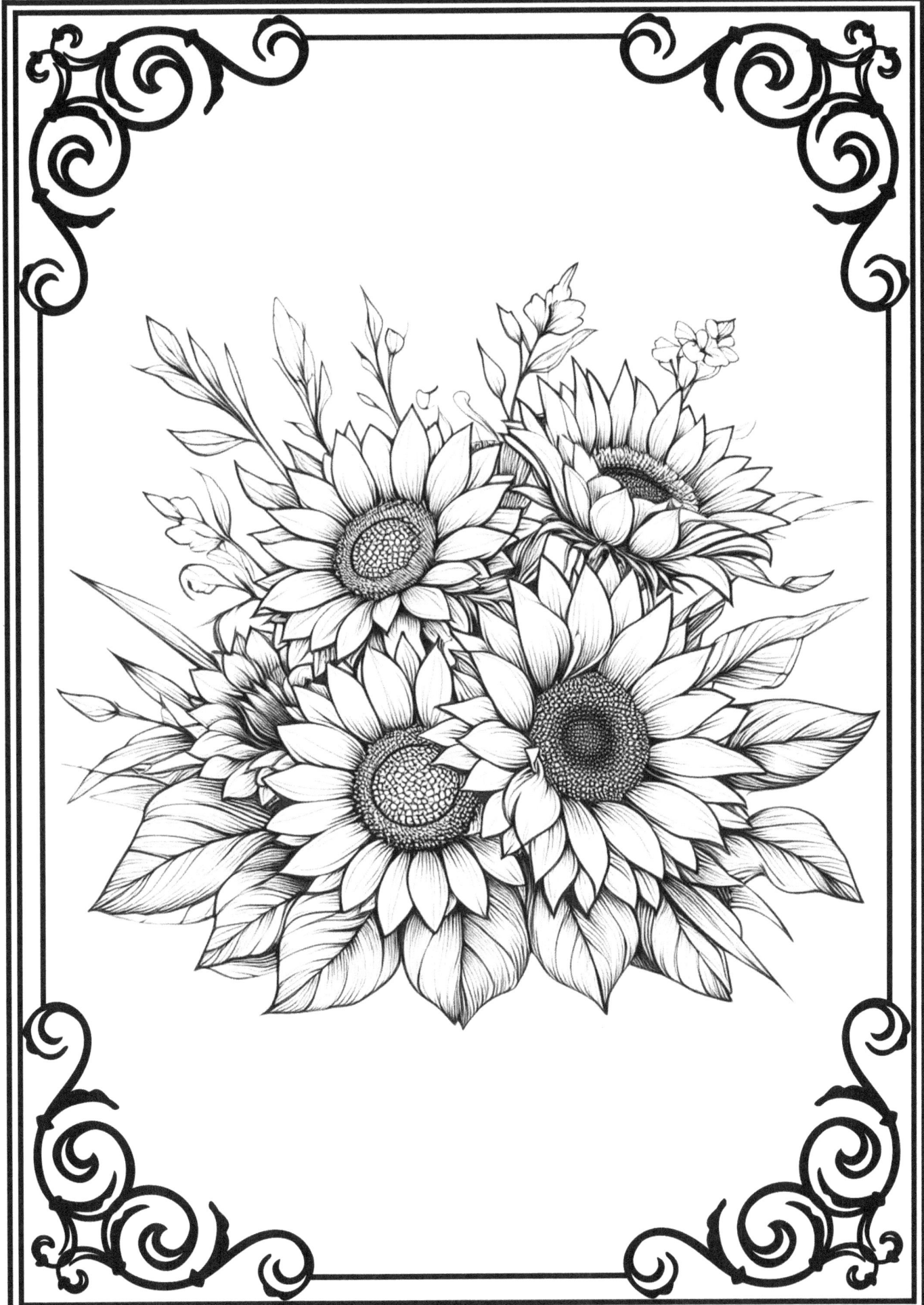

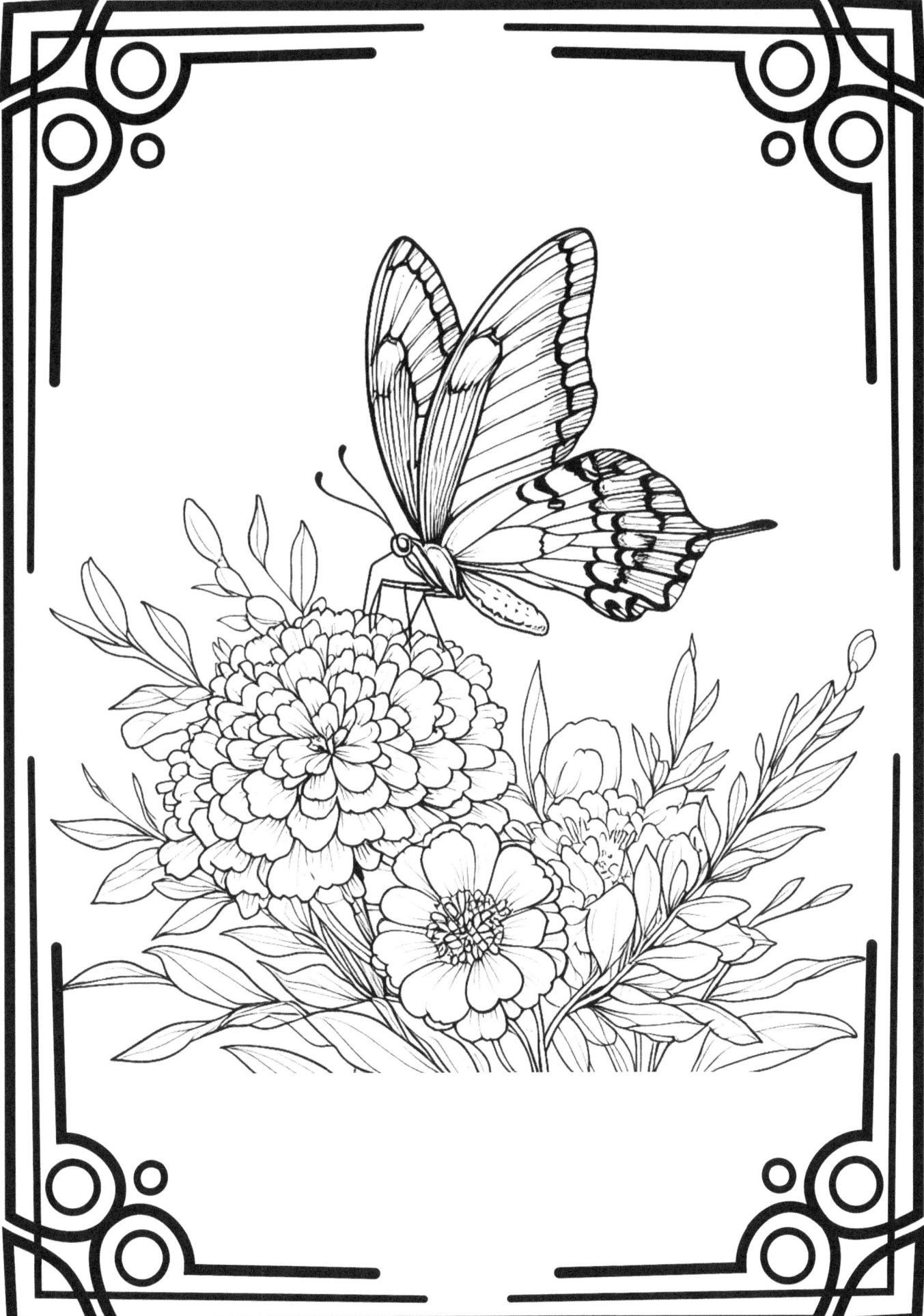

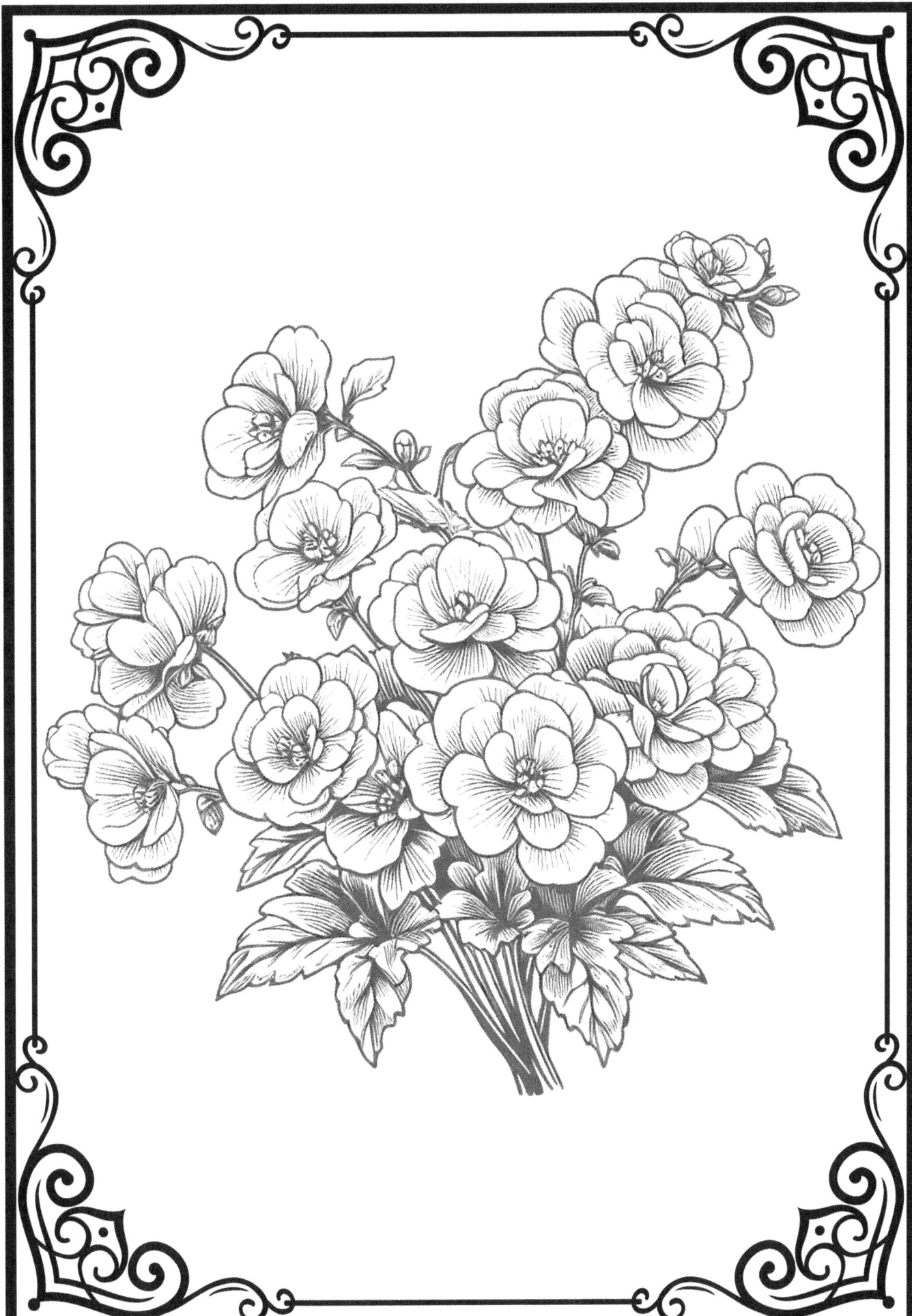

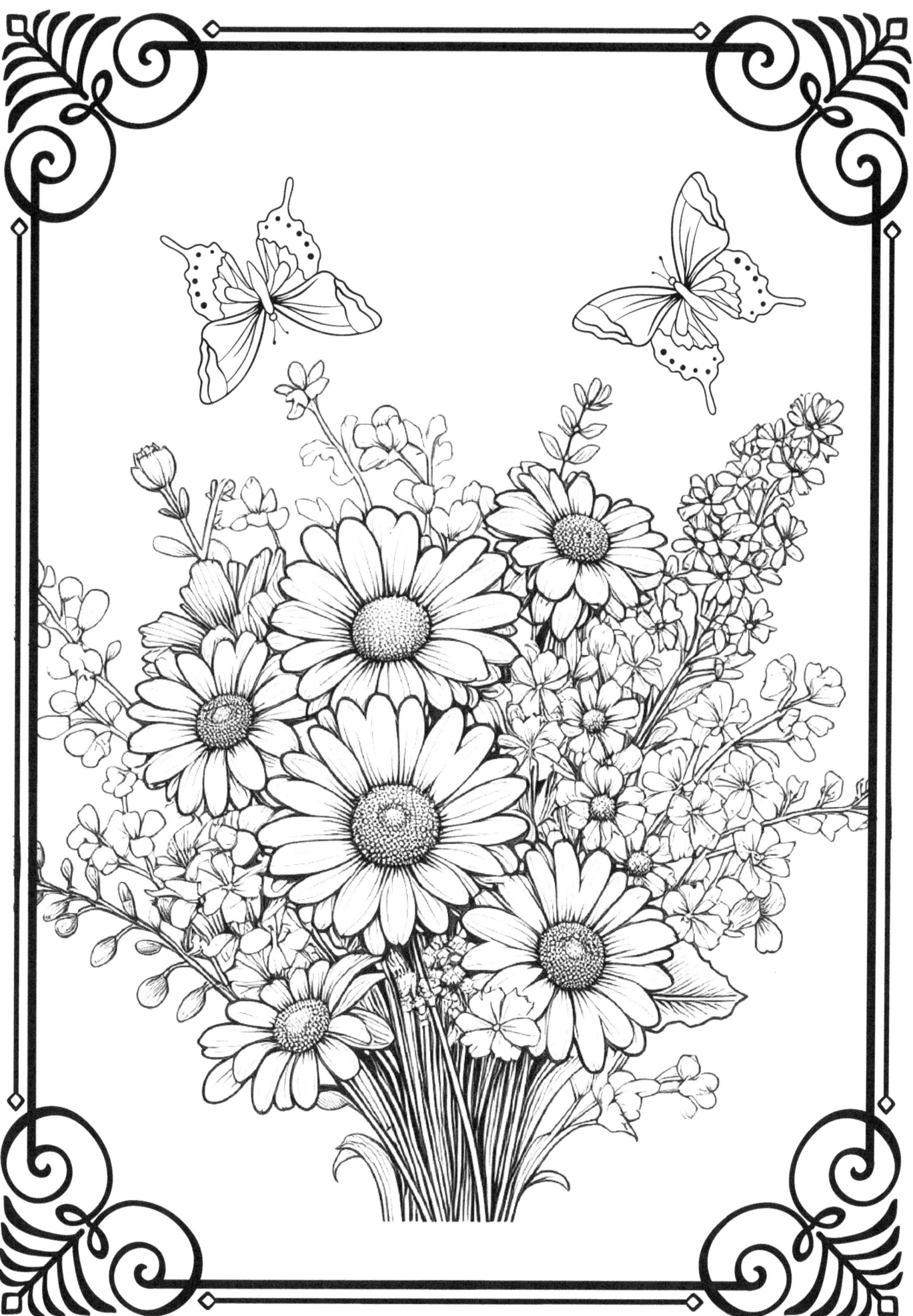

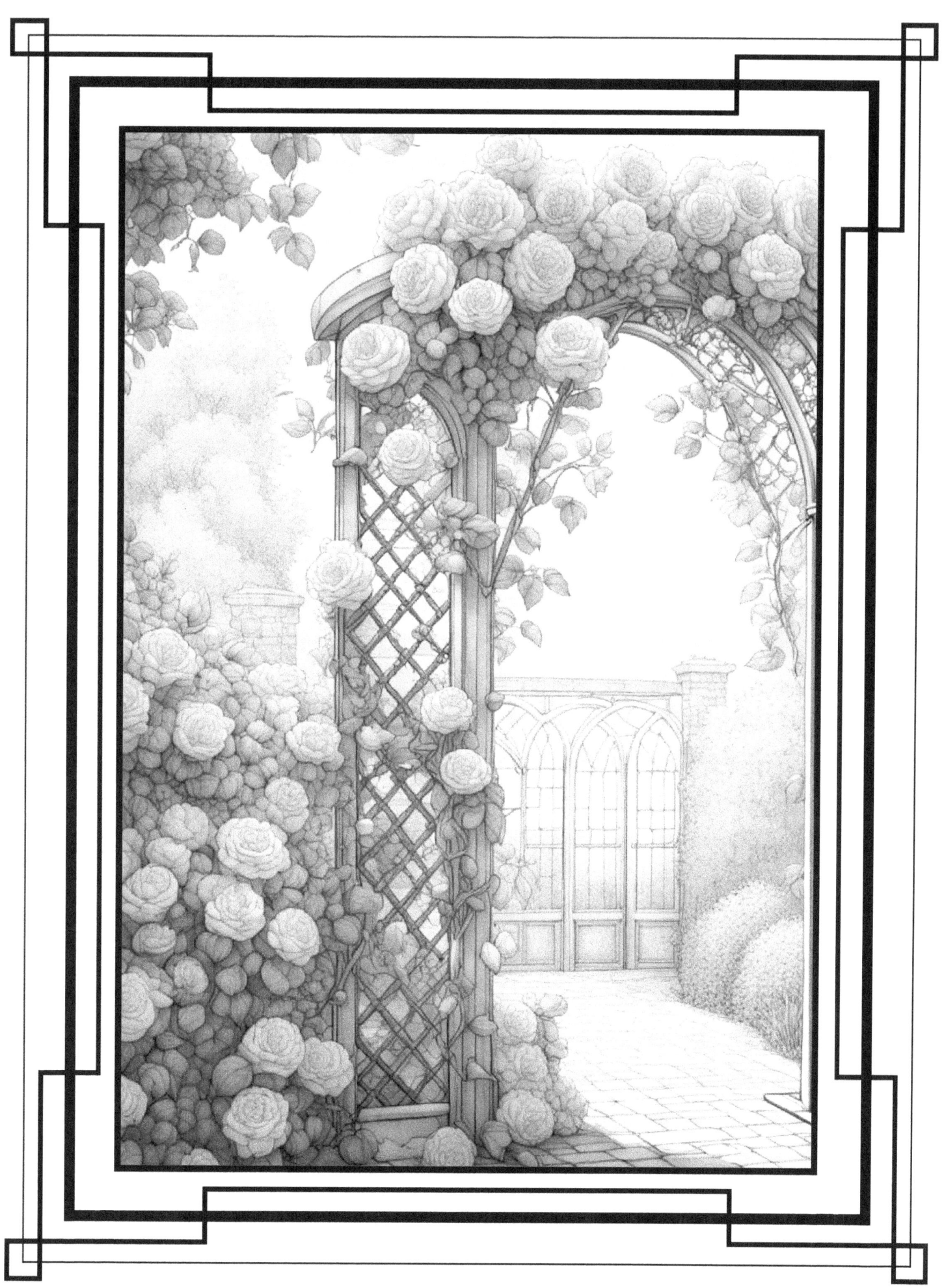